W9-ADR-069

GHOSTS
of The World

GHOSTS
of The World

Diane Canwell & Jonathan Sutherland

CHARTWELL
BOOKS, INC.

Published in 2008 by
CHARTWELL BOOKS, INC.
A division of BOOK SALES, INC.
114 Northfield Avenue
Edison, New Jersey 08837
USA

**Copyright © 2007 Regency
House Publishing Limited**
Niall House
24–26 Boulton Road
Stevenage, Hertfordshire
SG1 4QX, UK

For all editorial enquiries please contact
Regency House Publishing at
www.regencyhousepublishing.com

ISBN-13: 978-0-7858-2282-0

ISBN-10: 0-7858-2282-8

Printed in China

CONTENTS

INTRODUCTION – 10

CHAPTER ONE
CLASSIC CASES – 34

CHAPTER TWO
FAMOUS GHOSTS – 54

CHAPTER THREE
HAUNTED PLACES – 94

CHAPTER FOUR
GHOSTLY CREATURES – 158

CHAPTER FIVE
GHOSTLY TALES & LEGENDS – 176

CHAPTER SIX
GHOSTLY MESSAGES – 198

CHAPTER SEVEN
GHOSTLY PHENOMENA – 206

CHAPTER EIGHT
POLTERGEISTS – 242

INDEX – 250

INTRODUCTION

*H*ave you ever fancied you saw something strange and inexplicable out of the corner of your eye? Do you ever get the sense that you are not alone or that the temperature of the room has suddenly fallen? Perhaps you are not alone and perhaps, like many thousands of people across the centuries, you have experienced something that just cannot be explained.

Many believe that ghosts, or shadows from the past, make themselves known to living people, and that events that happened long ago are re-enacted in

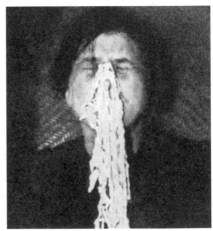

OPPOSITE LEFT: Could this be an apparition, or merely a clever camera trick?

OPPOSITE RIGHT: The medium, Eva C., with ectoplasm issuing from her facial orifices, photographed on 8 March 1918.

LEFT: Tony O'Rahilly photographed this fire at Wem Town Hall, Shropshire, England, on 19 November 1995, which, when developed, revealed what appears to be a ghostly child. Some think it is connected with a fire that gutted Wem in 1667, caused when a girl accidentally set fire to a thatched roof with a candle.

response to an unknown trigger.

Can the thousands of people claiming to have seen apparitions all be wrong? Or are they merely more suggestible than others? How can it be that people from different walks of life and from different parts of the world can, unprompted, all experience the same phenomenon associated with a particular place?

Sometimes visual clues come from the phenomena themselves, in that apparitions often seem unaware of our presence, and do not appear to notice that doors have been bricked in, that floor levels have been changed, or

Hatfield House, in Hertfordshire, was the home for a time of Elizabeth I, before she became Queen of England. It is haunted by a phantom coach and horses, which enters the house and proceeds up the stairs.

indeed that a building associated with them in life has been demolished or even moved.

From the grandest, most historic buildings in the world to humble shacks, unexplained presences have been recorded everywhere. Not everyone can experience them, however, and some continue to elude even those who are sensitive and attuned to the phenomenon. Ghosts, moreover, do not always fit the stereotype of the transparent figure, hovering a few inches above the ground. Some manifest themselves as a strong and insistent feeling, while others have the power to move physical objects. Very few interact

these pages, and many of the hauntings relate to historical figures or even celebrities, from Anne Boleyn to Elvis Presley. Then there are the classic cases, the ones that continue to intrigue, but which have never been explained.

But among the tales of kings, queens, nobles and celebrities are the more mundane but nevertheless remarkable accounts: the ghosts and apparitions of victims, suicides, murderers and even witches. The term 'ghost' derives from an ancient word meaning guest, so even if we believe in the phenomenon, and

OPPOSITE LEFT: This picture was cleverly created by repeatedly exposing a photographic plate or film to light.

OPPOSITE RIGHT & LEFT: Many famous people, separated by hundreds of years, have been connected with strange manifestations. These include such disparate figures as Anne Boleyn and Elvis Presley.

BELOW: This picture, another case of double exposure, was taken c.1905 by G.S. Smallwood of Chicago, and shows a girl flanked by two 'sprits'.

to any great extent with the living, and examples of those that do have often proved to be fraudulent.

Are we experiencing time slips? Are we seeing a re-run of something that happened in a particular place or situation many decades or centuries ago? Can we explain why the ghosts of those that are dying appear to their loved ones at the point of death? What do the odd orb-like objects, that cast light in the darkness or make unexplained noises, signify?

Some of the most famous cases from around the world are featured within

This is the site of a large henge and several stone circles that surround the Wiltshire village of Avebury in England. It is one of the largest and finest of Europe's Neolithic monuments, and is around 5,000 years old.

In 1916, a woman was standing on one of the earthen mounds, looking towards Avebury. Her view, however, was obscured by a village fair, that was currently in progress, in which booths and rides were being enjoyed by many people. The woman watched for a while, but drove off in her car when it started to rain. Later she discovered that no fair had been held in Avebury since 1850.

OPPOSITE: Places that have had a long and turbulent history, such as ancient castles, are often connected with ghostly activities, or are those claiming to have observed such phenomena merely letting their imaginations run away with them.

LEFT: The famous Brown Lady of Raynham, photographed on 19 September 1936 at Raynham Hall, Norfolk, England. A man, about to take a picture of the house's interior, was suddenly aware of an indistinct figure moving down the staircase, and immediately photograhed it. Some, however, believe the image was contrived.

can claim to have experienced it, we should never be concerned.

There have been many attempts to explain what a ghost actually is. Is it a manifestation or reincarnation of ourselves as we may have been or will be in another life? Is it the result of an intensely emotional situation or conflict? Are ghosts truly disembodied spirits that have somehow become separated from their mortal remains? Or do ghosts come from the realms of our subconscious, projected as images for others to see? It is even possible that what we are seeing is the next phase of existence following death.

Threave Castle, in Dumfriesshire, Scotland, stands on an island in the middle of the River Dee near to Castle Douglas. It was once the stronghold of the infamous Black Douglases, most notably Archibald the Grim. The appeal of visiting the castle is the short trip by boat, when the ferryman is sure to tell his passengers about the castle's ghosts, one of which is a phantom whisperer.

Exeter Cathedral, in England, is reputed to be haunted by three ghosts: that of a nun, who appears during July at around 1900 hours, but quickly disappears once seen; a monk that has been reported as frequenting the area surrounding the cathedral; and most bizarre of all, a strange apparition which is said to have three heads.

But how can we explain all the different kinds of manifestations, from apparitions that could pass for living people to those that appear to be headless or even worse. How can ghostly trains, ships and cars be simply explained away, and what of the plethora of phantom hounds of hell, bears, horses – even the great ape that is reputed to haunt a Scottish castle.

Most ancient buildings, and even some modern ones, from the catacombs beneath the city of Paris to the bizarre Winchester Mansion in California, still hold unexplained secrets. Legends are passed down from generation to generation, from the story of the weeping woman of Santa Fe to Europe's

BELOW: This photograph was taken inside
Newby Church, near Ripon, North
Yorkshire, by the then vicar, Rev. K.F Lord,
in the early 1960s. He did not see the ghost
when taking the photograph, but it showed
up clearly once the film was developed.

in the Second World War, to the
phantom Maori canoe that presaged a
major volcanic eruption.

odd and puzzling radiant boys. Were the
rulers of Prussia and Germany indeed
truly cursed, whenever the White Lady
appeared, and did a pact exist between
Lady Beresford and Lord Tyrone that
transcended life and death? Here, the
true story of *The Exorcist* can be told,
also that of the Bell Witch of Tennessee;
of the poltergeist that cursed a young
woman from Nova Scotia, so that she
lived her life as an arsonist and outcast;
and of another that could be said to
have murdered its victim.

It seems that it is possible for the
paranormal to attach itself to
inanimate objects, from the USS
Hornet, whose crew served so gallantly

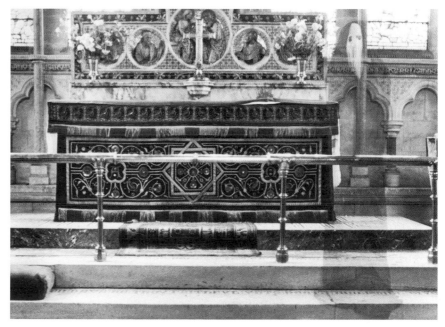

25

Sacred to Memory
of

ELIZABETH WHITE ROBERTSON
second daughter of
GILBERT ROBERTSON late
Superintendent of agriculture
Norfolk Island who died January 1st
1847, aged 24 years.

Thou art gone to the grave but we will not deplore thee
Though sorrows and darkness encompass the tomb
The Saviour has passed through its portal before thee
And the lamp of his love is thy guide through the gloom.

INTRODUCTION

RIGHT: Derek Stafford photographed the floodlit church at Prestbury, near Cheltenham in England, on 22 November 1990, and later found this hooded figure on the last slide. A 'Black Abbot' is said to haunt the churchyard.

BELOW: This photograph of her children's grave was taken by a mother in around 1947. When developed, it was noticed that an image of a child had appeared, which was of neither of the children buried there. No pictures of children had been taken, so a double exposure was out of the question.

OPPOSITE BELOW RIGHT: A close-up of a photograph taken in Staffordshire, England, on 4 March 1993. Brenda Ray did not notice the figure in the black cape when she took the picture, and it doesn't appear on the next frame.

LEFT: At a séance conducted by the Polish medium, Franek Klushi, in Warsaw on 25 November 1919, a materialized spirit can be seen standing behind him.

BELOW: Ghostly sightings are not only confined to people, but can also be of animals.

A degree of skepticism must inevitably be attached to a subject such as this. What cannot be denied, however, is that many objective witnesses give identical descriptions of what they have seen, which cannot easily be ignored. The alternative explanation is that they were experiencing a mass hallucination, triggered by identical stimuli.

Many of these stories have inevitably done the rounds, and over time have become vastly distorted or embellished, while others have been researched to such a degree that a plausible conclusion has been reached in which everything makes sense – barring, of course, the ghost itself.

The Eiffel Tower, that stands on the Champ de Mars beside the River Seine, is an immense structure of exposed iron latticework supports, which was erected for the Paris Exposition of 1889. Its construction, however, provoked strong reactions from some of the leading figures of the day, such as Émile Zola, Guy de Maupassant and Alexandre Dumas the Younger, who regarded it as monstrous, useless, and an affront to good taste.

It is said that a young man took his girlfriend to the top of the tower with the intention of proposing marriage to her. But she turned him down and he threw her from the tower to her death. Visitors to the tower at night have reported hearing a girl laughing and saying NO, followed by a scream, then silence.

Durham Castle, in England, was built by the Normans in the 11th century to protect the Bishop of Durham from attack from the English population in the north, who were still resentful and unsettled following the Norman Conquest of England in 1066. It is an excellent example of the early motte and bailey castles favoured by the Normans.

The castle is reportedly haunted by the wife of one of the former Prince Bishops of Durham, whose ghost has been seen on the back staircase, down which she fell and broke her neck.

CHAPTER ONE
CLASSIC CASES

IMOGEN: A VICTORIAN GHOST STORY

In England in the 1860s, a large Victorian house, thereafter to be known as Garden Reach, was built in Cheltenham, Gloucestershire. The first to occupy the house was the Swinhoe family, but Mrs. Swinhoe died soon afterwards and her husband, Henry, appears to have turned to alcohol for solace. After two years, Henry Swinhoe remarried, and his new wife, Imogen, was also a heavy drinker. Henry may possibly have introduced her to alcohol, but in any case both were quarrelsome and abusive drunks.

The fact that Henry had hidden the original Mrs. Swinhoe's jewellery somewhere in the house seems to have been a major cause of the arguments. Imogen believed that the jewellery should be hers, but it was Henry's intention to keep it for the children of his first marriage, so that they would be well provided for in later life.

Imogen eventually left Henry, and died of alcoholism shortly afterwards.

Inexplicably, her body was brought back to Cheltenham and she was buried in a graveyard not far from the house. Henry himself also died soon after and the house was sold to an elderly couple. The husband lasted for only six months and his widow moved out of the house, leaving it empty for about five years. Captain F.W. Despard began to rent Garden Reach in April

Cheltenham Spa, in Gloucestershire, is England's most complete Regency town. It is conveniently placed for visiting the Cotswolds, Stratford-upon-Avon and Bath.

1882, bringing his second wife, his large family, and several servants to live with him in the house. The hauntings began the following June.

The captain's eldest daughter, Rosina, was certainly no fool, and would later go on to qualify as a doctor and have an impressive career. Now in her 20s, however, she seemed destined to be the principal witness to the subsequent manifestations that began to occur: what is also striking about Rosina is that she handled what ensued with supreme equanimity.

It all started when Rosina heard a noise outside her bedroom door one night, but when she opened it, no one was there. Rosina stepped into the hallway and looked towards the stairs, at the top of which, though shrouded in darkness, stood a tall woman dressed completely in black. Rosina watched the figure walk down the stairs and followed it for as long as the tiny candle she was holding allowed. Her later description of the event was full of useful detail: the apparition's face was covered by a handkerchief and her left hand was hidden inside the sleeve of her dress. The apparition, more remarkably, was not transparent and appeared to be very solid indeed. Rosina also noted that subsequent appearances followed no particular pattern, but could occur at any time of the day or night.

At least half-a-dozen other people in the household, including family and servants, also saw the ghost, but the captain and his wife did not. In fact, Rosina often saw the ghost enter the room where her father and stepmother were sitting and was amazed that they seemed oblivious of the fact. At the time, the rumour spread that the figure was no ghost at all, simply the captain's mistress, although this was patently untrue.

Rosina tried to photograph the figure on a number of occasions and even tried to test its solidity, by tying string across the stairs; but the apparition walked right through it, leaving the string undisturbed. Rosina even attempted to touch the ghost, but the figure simply receded, slipping out of her grasp each time. She tried to talk to it, and except for making a slight gasping noise, the ghost seemed unable to speak.

Over the years, the apparition began to fade from view until, by 1889, only its footsteps could be heard. The haunting was thoroughly investigated by the Society for Psychical Research, which regarded Rosina's journal of her sightings to be one of the best-recorded it had ever seen. The general opinion was that it was the ghost of Imogen Swinhoe, searching for the jewels she still regarded as rightfully hers.

In around 1892 the Despards moved out of the house, but there were to be later sightings. In October 1958, John Thorne, living in a house nearby, woke to find a strange woman in his bedroom. His description of the figure matched the one that Rosina had given 70 years before. Thorne's brother William and his own teenage son also saw the apparition on several different occasions.

Strangely, however, when William Thorne came across the original report of the Cheltenham hauntings, he realized that he had not in fact seen Imogen Swinhoe, but Rosina Despard.

THE BLACKWALL TUNNEL

The Blackwall Tunnel in east London, then the longest underwater tunnel in the world, was opened on 22 May 1897. During its construction, which took six years to complete, 641 people living in Greenwich had to be rehoused because it was necessary for their homes to be demolished. The cost of this, including the purchase of the land and the building of the tunnel itself, came to around £1,400,000.

One of the demolished houses appears to have belonged to Sir Walter

Raleigh (1552–1618), an Elizabethan courtier, writer and explorer, and it is said that the first pipe of tobacco, smoked in England, was the one lit by Raleigh in that house. It was later inhabited by both Sir John de Pulteney (who was four times Lord Mayor of London) and by Sebastian Cabot, the Italian explorer and navigator.

At the time when the Blackwall Tunnel was being built, Brunel had only recently invented the tunnel-shield method, which though unwieldy, was regarded as very safe. It had been used on an earlier Thames tunnel and would also be used in the construction of the London Underground railway. There had been reports, a little before the

Blackwall Tunnel was begun, that men were being killed at the rate of one a month, during the construction of the Hudson River Tunnel, connecting Jersey City and Hoboken with New York City, but there were only seven fatalities in the six years of the Blackwall Tunnel's construction. As traffic through the tunnel increased, it was soon apparent

that a second tunnel was needed, which took seven years to construct.

In October 1972, a motorcyclist offered a lift to a boy from Essex, whom he saw hitchhiking on the Greenwich side of the Blackwall Tunnel. But by the time the other end was reached the boy had disappeared. The biker sped back to see if his passenger had fallen off, but could find nothing. He contacted the boy's family to tell them what had happened and was told that the boy had died in the tunnel several years earlier, while riding pillion on a motorbike.

EXHIBIT 22542

Given the vast number of exhibits on show in London's British Museum, it is rather surprising that only two major hauntings and one strangely inexplicable incident have been recorded.

The first haunting relates to exhibit 22542, an Egyptian mummy case. This is covered in hieroglyphics and bears the likeness of a beautiful singer, dedicated to the god Amun-Ra. It was discovered in the 1880s by British tourists, who bought it from a trader in Thebes, in Egypt. It is allegedly linked to at least 13 deaths, and one of the new owners was in fact injured in a hunting accident the very next day, necessitating his arm

being amputated, while the other vanished in a mysterious way and was never seen again.

After this, the one-armed man sold the case to a dealer in Cairo. Three other people bought the case after him, and all died, after which it was shipped to London. Here it was bought by a collector, who was warned that evil

OPPOSITE: The entrance to the Blackwell Tunnel.

LEFT: This is not 22542, but it is similar.

emanated from the case and that he should rid himself of it. The collector took this advice and sold it on to someone else, who had it photographed; the photographer died the following day.

It is said that when the photographs were developed, the expected image of a beautiful woman had changed to that of an old, evil woman, who appeared to be staring straight into the photographer's lens. After this, the case found its way into the home of a woman, but by the next morning, her pets had died and all the glass in her house had been unaccountably shattered. The woman herself, despite expert medical attention, fell into a deep, coma-like state. In a rare moment of lucidity, however, she disposed of the case, and her health was subsequently restored.

The mummy case found its final resting place in the British Museum in 1889, but the curse appeared to be still active. When two porters brought it into the building, one fell and broke his leg and the other died within the week. The case, by this time, had a great deal of notoriety attached to it, and it is said that artists could never draw it accurately. At night, museum caretakers constantly complained of an evil aura surrounding the case, and one claimed to have seen an apparition, which he described as that of a hideous yellowish-green wrinkled face. There was yet another photographer, who was reputed to have committed suicide after his photographs were developed.

When the body was eventually removed from its case and taken to America, it was said to have caused the sinking of the *Empress of Ireland* in St. Lawrence Bay. In 1921 two attempts were made to exorcise it, and the apparition that emerged was described

BELOW & OPPOSITE: The British Museum has the world's largest collection of Egyptian antiquities outside Cairo.

as having a flat, leering face and a jelly-like body. It is believed that the hieroglyphs signified powerful magic, that was activated after the body had been removed and therefore desecrated.

THE AFRICAN MASK

The second of the British Museum's hauntings relates to an African mask, that is said to cause deep wounds to appear on the body of anyone who touches it. There is no logical reason why it should do this, as it has no sharp edges, but it has led to the belief that a curse is attached to the object.

KATEBIT

To a lesser extent, the remains of Katebit, housed in the Egyptian Rooms of the British Museum, are said to be capable of movement. Katebit was a priestess of the god Amun-Ra, and witnesses have reported seeing her head move from side to side.

BORLEY RECTORY

Built close to the River Stour in Essex, Borley Rectory was constructed in 1863, to house the Reverend Henry D.E. Bull, his wife, and 14 children, on a site that already had a significant history. The Doomsday Book told of the existence of a Borley Manor prior to 1066, and a wooden church was probably also built at that time. Beneath the foundations ran underground tunnels and a complex of vaulted rooms. The most popular

BELOW: Borley Rectory, photographed in 1929 before it was gutted by fire. It was known as 'the most haunted house in England'.

OPPOSITE: The church at Borley.

story was that in 1362 a Benedictine monastery was built on the site, which would explain the strange story connected with Borley of a monk who had fallen in love with a nun from a nearby convent. They intended to elope, but their plan was discovered, and a friend, who was to have helped them to escape in a carriage, was beheaded. The monk was hanged and the nun was bricked up alive in one of the vaults.

By 1875 the Reverend Bull had extended the rectory and the first

paranormal activities became apparent around 1885, when a ghostly nun was seen staring through the window into the dining room. This happened on so many occasions that the Bulls decided to brick up the window.

The Reverend Bull died in May 1892 and his position was inherited by his son, another Henry. The nun was seen again in July 1900, as was a phantom coach, while others witnessed several manifestations of the monk and nun together. The nun was wearing a grey

cloak and the monk was tonsured and dressed in a long, black gown.

The second Henry died in 1927 and for several months the building was left empty. The Reverend Smith moved in October 1928, and soon after began to hear voices calling 'Carlos', which was the nickname of the first Henry Bull. Pebbles were thrown at windows, lights were turned on and off, footsteps were heard, and a phantom coach was seen coming through the rectory gates.

Harry Price, the famous psychic investigator, arrived on the scene in June 1929. He and a reporter from the *Daily Times* witnessed stones and

objects being thrown around a room and the sound of bells ringing. By the middle of July the Smiths had had as much as they could take and moved out. Again the house lay empty, this time until October 1930.

The Reverend Foyster was the next to take up residence, but it was his wife, Marianne, who would experience the most bizarre occurrences. During the period October 1930 to October 1935 no fewer than 2,000 poltergeist phenomena were witnessed. The second Henry Bull was now seen, glass objects were broken, and books were thrown across rooms, as were pebbles and an iron. An exorcism was attempted, but obviously failed, since Marianne was thrown out of bed that very night. By 1935 the Foysters had also had enough and the house lay empty for at least two years. This, however, failed to stay the hand of the poltergeist.

Price decided to lease the house himself and began a year-long study of the place in June 1937. He was aware of a chilly atmosphere in certain rooms, but he never saw the nun. After Price had completed his investigations, Captain Gregson and his family bought the building, but on 27 February 1939 it was gutted by a fire, when it was

claimed that phantom figures could be seen staring out of the windows as the house burned. Eventually, everything that remained was demolished in 1944.

THE MONKS OF ST. BRUNO

In France, in the middle of the 13th century, King Louis IX decided to give a house in Paris to the Order of St. Bruno, and six monks accordingly moved into the building. The house, built by King Robert, was located close to the Palace of Vauvert, but had lain empty for several years.

No sooner had the monks moved in than the manifestations began. People began to see lights at the windows, screams and howls were heard, and a green man, with a long, white beard, began to attack passersby.

As the palace was still owned by the king, he sent a group of commissioners to investigate, but another development will have skeptics rolling their eyes in disbelief. The St. Bruno monks said that they would deal with the manifestations themselves, provided the king gave them the palace as their new permanent home. As soon as the deeds were drawn up, giving the building over to the monks, the hauntings unsurprisingly ceased. Although this was a famous and

notorious case in its time, it was clearly one of the earliest cases where a so-called haunting was used to achieve fraudulent ends.

THE SHACK (HYDESVILLE RAPPINGS)

Located in the hamlet of Hydesville in New York State, a tiny shack became the scene of strange phenomena, but before it came to be the home of the Fox family, it had been occupied by a succession of tenants for many years, who had used it as a temporary dwelling while looking for more permanent homes.

The last of these tenants were the Weekmans, and although John Fox did not know it, they had been witnesses to strange happenings. Rapping sounds had been heard and the Weekmans's eight-year-old daughter had been woken by a cold hand touching her face, terrifying her so much that she could neither move nor scream. From then on the child refused to sleep in the room, leading the family to seek alternative accommodation.

The experiences of the Fox family began on 31 March 1848. They began to hear rapping sounds and it was soon apparent that the two daughters,

Margaret (15) and Kate (12), were communicating with the spirit, that obeyed the girls when they commanded it to stop rapping.

Also involved in the story was their brother, David, who did not live in the house but was eager to decode the rapping and discover what the spirit was trying to say, and their elder sister, Leah, who lived in Rochester. They subsequently learned from a neighbour that it was possibly the spirit of Charles Rosma, whose body appeared to have been buried beneath the house. A full skeleton was never found, but it is believed that fragments of bone and hair were later found.

Sightseers began to throng to the house, wishing to share the mysterious phenomena for themselves. Ultimately the children went to live with Leah in Rochester, but the spirit simply

OPPOSITE: Ghosts can appear in both grand houses and derelict shacks, such as this one on Prince Edward Island, Canada.

BELOW: Margaret and Kate became mediums like these, but later admitted to making the whole thing up.

followed them there. Leah hit on a way of making money out of the situation and booked a hall, charging $1 to

45

BELOW: Fort McNair, in Washington, D.C., is more than 200 years old.

OPPOSITE & PAGES 48–49: Jamaica, the home in the 1700s of the White Witch of Jamaica, the notorious Annie Palmer.

enter. Of the people that arrived, no one was disappointed and many heard the rappings for themselves. Doctors started to become interested in the case in 1850 and decided that the noise was coming from the girls themselves. They were accordingly made to sit with their feet stretched out and separated by cushions. The rappings stopped, but when the cushions were removed, the rappings immediately resumed.

Margaret and Kate went on to become mediums, charging a fee for public séances and extra for private ones; they also became skilled at mirror writing.

In October 1888, however, Margaret admitted that the whole thing had been a fraud, and that the sounds had been made with their knee joints. By this time, both were poor and addicted to drink, but later, Margaret retracted her confession, and to this day no one can be sure what actually did occur.

BUILDING 20

Fort McNair was originally established on a point of land where the Potomac and Anacostia rivers join. The first buildings were thrown up in 1794, and more land to the north was purchased in 1826 to build the first Federal penitentiary; a hospital was built next to it in 1857.

The penitentiary itself was where Mary Surratt, and the other conspirators found guilty of the plot to assassinate President Abraham Lincoln, were hanged. Bizarrely, as we shall see, it was information supplied by Mary Surratt's son that helped to condemn his own mother to death.

John Surratt Jr. had been a Confederate messenger, carrying information regarding the movement

of Union troop during the Civil War. He was introduced to John Wilkes Booth in December 1864 and agreed to help him in his plot to kill the president. He subsequently colluded in what some claimed to have been a failed attempt to kidnap Lincoln in March 1865.

Surratt's whereabouts on the night when John Wilkes Booth fatally shot the president on 14 April 1865, at Ford's Theatre in Washington, D.C., is open to speculation. Surratt claimed he was in New York, and that he fled to Canada on hearing the news of the assassination. He was still in hiding there when his mother was hanged on 7 July 1865.

For his mother, however, it had been an altogether different story. There are rumours to this day that many of the so-called conspirators had been framed in an attempt to hide the real truth. But regardless of this, Mary Surratt's life ended only a few yards from where Building 21 of Fort McNair now stands.

The building next door held all the conspirators who were tried and sentenced to death. Mary Surratt's cell was located on the third floor of Building 20, where a presence could undoubtedly be felt, while the window continually rattled, as though someone

were trying to get in or out of the room. Over the years, several witnesses claim to have heard a sobbing sound, rather like the noise made by a high wind in an enclosed space.

THE WHITE WITCH OF JAMAICA

Rose Hall was once the home of the so-called White Witch of Jamaica, and stood at the centre of one of the largest sugar plantations on the island. It is haunted by the ghost of Annie Palmer, who was white in the ethnical sense, and was born in France. Annie terrorized the

slaves who worked on her plantation, ruling them with a rod of iron. Perceived defiance or insolence of any kind was punished with public whippings, torture, and even death. She even took slaves as lovers, murdering them when she got tired of them and is said to have killed her own husband.

Some say Annie was killed by her slave overseer, a man steeped in voodoo lore, and that Annie used magical powers of her own for a while to keep herself from harm. But when Annie killed the fiancé of the overseer's

daughter, after he had been forced to pleasure her, a supernatural battle was fought between overseer and mistress that Annie eventually lost. Voodoo rituals were performed at her burial, but were followed imprecisely so that her spirit continues to return.

Mediums raised a terror-stricken spirit, when they attempted to contact her, which would not depart despite repeated exorcisms.

THE PIANO

On the corner of Rue Racine and Avenue Montaigne, in a suburb of Paris, is an elegant three-storey mansion, built in the 1860s. It was originally used by Napoleon III, and was later the property of the actor and film producer, Robert Lamoureux.

In 1949 a diplomat, working at the American embassy in Paris, rented the house, and he, his wife and their four children moved in. Shortly afterwards, however, the diplomat was called away on business, which is when the strange occurrences began.

The wife began to hear music played in the early hours of the morning. At first, she fancied it was coming from outside, before realizing that it was in fact coming from downstairs; however,

she was too afraid to take a look. The same thing happened the following night and continued night after night thereafter. She closed the piano lid and left out open music sheets, but every night the same music continued to be played. The husband eventually returned, learning all that had occurred.

Talking with a neighbour one day, the diplomat's wife heard how they were being woken up by a hunting horn, and gradually the story was pieced together. It seems that Napoleon had installed a mistress in the house, and having tired of her, left her alone with her piano. One of the American couple's children, in the presence of their maid, also reported seeing a lady in the corner of that same room.

The house was eventually acquired by property developers and by the late 1960s had deteriorated into a grievous state of disrepair. A psychic investigator visited the house just before it was pulled down, and claims to have seen flickering lights and other odd shapes moving on the staircase.

THE WHITE LADY OF WOLFSEGG

One would rather have expected a 12th-century fortified castle to be haunted,

and the castle at Wolfsegg in Bavaria, that overlooks the River Danube, does not disappoint. It was built in 1028 and belonged to a succession of noble families until 1918, some of which could best be described as robber barons, who preyed on the wayfarers who passed through their lands.

The victims of a triple murder, that probably took place in the 14th century, still haunt the castle, together with the ghost of the young wife of the then owner, who was caught in flagrante delicto by her husband, subsequently to be killed by the lover's relations. One of these stories may explain the archetypal White Lady of Wolfsegg and the fact that she still roams the castle's corridors.

STRANGE PARALLELS

One of the few cases to yield credible photographic evidence is that of the so-called ghostly monks of Aetna Springs, California, an area which nowadays has largely been given over to a golf course.

The ghosts of eight monks, dressed in white robes, their faces contorted with pain, have been seen walking on the golf course. Some believe they are Dominican friars, who were tortured to death by rival Franciscans.

The Spanish Franciscans were notorious for their cruel treatment of local Native Americans, in their efforts to convert them, and Dominicans are thought to have attemped to save them. Images of these ghostly monks are striking, in that their robes appear to be on fire. They are believed to have been executed by burning, having possibly been tortured and crucified before their deaths.

Strange parallels also exist in Napa County, where Aetna Springs is also located. It will be remembered that the Reverend Sun Myung Moon's Unification Church used to operate here from the 1970s to the 1990s. There is no longer a connection with either the Dominicans or Moon's sect, but spirits are undoubtedly wandering in the area after nearly 500 years.

RIGHT: The castle at Wolfsegg overlooks the River Danube in Bavaria.

PAGES 52 & 53: Harvard University in Cambridge, Massachusetts, has its fair share of ghosts. Thayer Hall, once a textile mill, is haunted by ghosts in Victorian dress that pass through doors that have long ceased to exist.

CHAPTER TWO
FAMOUS GHOSTS

LADY MARY HOWARD

Lady Mary Howard, who lived in the 17th century, was destined never to find peace, either in life or death. She was the daughter of John Fitz, a man corrupted by extreme wealth, which led to the murder of two men in Tavistock, on the borders of Dartmoor, England.

Mary soon found herself hated as a result of her father's activities and she was only nine when her father committed suicide after becoming insane at the age of 30. Having inherited this wealth, Mary was forced by King James I to marry Sir Alan Percy, when she was only 12.

Sir Alan was the first of four husbands whom Mary would outlive. Percy died of pneumonia, leaving her free to marry Thomas Darcy, a man she truly loved. Sadly he died within months of the marriage. Her next two husbands were desperate to get their hands on her money, but Mary was canny and made sure that most of it remained concealed.

When her fourth husband died, Mary returned to Fitzford House, the family pile, which had lain deserted since the death of her father; but Mary was now returning to it with her beloved son, George. She hoped to live a peaceful life there at last, but a few months later George died and Mary, her heart broken, died exactly a month later. Unfortunately for Mary's memory, her evil father and the deaths

BELOW: Okehampton Castle in Devon, where the ghost of Mary Howard performs its never-ending task.

OPPOSITE: Dartmoor, Devon, near to where Mary's father, John Fitz, was involved in a double murder.

of her husbands, for which she was inevitably blamed, have contributed to the creation of a legend. Tales

Windsor Castle, the largest in Britain, has been a royal residence since the reign of William I in the 11th century. It was rebuilt by Edward III in the 13th century, and further improvements have been made by successive monarchs.

The castle has a plethora of ghostly tales to tell, of suicide, witchcraft and demonic possession. The legendary spirit of Herne the Hunter is often seen galloping his horse through Windsor Great Park, accompanied by his pack of hounds. In life, Herne was the favourite huntsman of Richard II, and having saved his king from being killed by a stag, was mortally wounded himself. A local wizard cured Herne by magical means, which meant attaching the dead animal's antlers to his head. In return, however, Herne had to forfeit his hunting skills, to which he agreed. This great loss, however, eventually sent him mad. One day, he hung himself from an oak tree, the antlers still affixed to his head.

Another famous ghost is reputedly that of Henry VIII, and Henry's second wife, Anne Boleyn, whom he had beheaded, has been seen looking out of a window in the Dean's Cloister. She always wears a black gown with a black lace shawl covering her shoulders.

throughout the county of Devon tell of a phantom coach, made bizarrely from the bones of Mary's four husbands. Countless people claim to have seen the coach, travelling towards Okehampton Castle, where Mary's ghost is doomed to pick a blade of grass from the castle grounds every night, until not a single one remains.

AARON BURR

Aaron Burr was born in New Jersey in 1756. His family produced a number of famous clergymen, but their profession held scant appeal as far as Aaron was concerned. He studied law instead, preached independence, and served in the rebel army against the British during the American Revolution. He very nearly became President of the United States, losing the contest to Thomas Jefferson. He became vice president, but developed an almost rabid dislike of Alexander Hamilton.

The feeling was mutual and though Hamilton had little love for Jefferson himself, his hatred for Aaron was even stronger. Hamilton sided with Jefferson, which cost Aaron his chance of becoming president. Ultimately, the rivalry would end in bloodshed.

Hamilton and Burr fought a duel on 11 July 1804, in which Hamilton was fatally wounded; he was rushed to New York, where he died several days later. As duelling was illegal, Aaron was forced to flee after warrants were signed for his arrest. Even though

Hamilton was dead, he still had powerful friends who hated Burr almost as much.

It is also worth mentioning that 27 Jane Street, in Greenwich Village, where Hamilton died, has been the centre of poltergeist activity in the past.

Burr was eventually forced to flee the United States, but was persuaded to return in 1814 by his daughter, Theodosia. His ship was due to dock in New York, where she was due to meet him, and with this in mind, Theodosia boarded a ship, which was lost in a

OPPOSITE ABOVE: Thomas Jefferson (1743–1826), the third U.S. president.

OPPOSITE BELOW: Jane St., where Alexander Hamilton eventually died.

BELOW: Cape Hatteras and its famous lighthouse.

storm off Cape Hatteras, North Carolina. Her ghost can still be seen, wandering on the shoreline.

Burr was able to settle back down in New York and at the ripe age of 77 married Eliza Jumel in 1833. She was a wealthy woman, 20 years his junior, and had a colourful past. She had once been penniless, but had married Stephen Jumel, a rich New Yorker. It was rumoured that Eliza had murdered him and that his ghost haunted the mansion that he had built.

Eliza and Burr married shortly after she was widowed, but they were divorced within a year, only a handful of days before Burr himself died at the age of 78. The Jumel mansion in New York City continued to be Eliza's home, and she died there at the age of 93 in 1865. The ghost of an old woman sometimes appears on the balcony of this magnificent building, and she can often be seen scaring children away.

ABRAHAM LINCOLN

It is not surprising, given his violent death and the indelible imprint he made on American society and history, that Abraham Lincoln should have lingered as a ghost. He lived at a time when spiritualism was popular:

Lincoln's wife was particularly interested in the subject, and when their son, William, died, Mary Todd Lincoln arranged for séances to be held in the White House. Abraham Lincoln attended some of these and it is said that a medium advised Lincoln during a particularly bad phase for the North, during the American Civil War.

Lincoln is reputed to have forseen his own murder in dreams, and ten days before he was assassinated, saw himself lying in a coffin. He also described his

LEFT: Abraham Lincoln (1809–1865).

BELOW: John Wilkes Booth assassinated President Lincoln on 14 April 1865.

OPPOSITE LEFT: Queen Wilhelmina of the Netherlands.

OPPOSITE RIGHT: The White House, where Lincoln's ghostly presence has often been felt or seen.

dream of being on board a ship to friends. Lincoln was not the only one to foresee his assassination at the hands of John Wilkes Booth on 14 April 1865, one of Lincoln's bodyguards, W.H. Crook, also begged the president not to attend the theatre that night.

Shortly after Lincoln's assassination, sounds of ghostly footsteps were reportedly heard in the White House, while Grace Coolidge, the wife of the 13th president, saw Lincoln's ghost staring out of the window of the Oval Office. During Roosevelt's presidency, Queen Wilhelmina of the Netherlands clearly saw Lincoln, wearing a top hat and standing in a doorway. When she recounted this to Roosevelt, he told her she was staying in Lincoln's room and that she was only one of many who claimed to have seen him.

Lincoln was seen sitting on the bed in the room, putting on his boots, and there is another report that his ghost had once attempted to set fire to the bed. President Harry Truman, although he never saw Lincoln's ghost, nevertheless felt his presence, and heard knocking on the door. Several fake spirit photographs were created after Lincoln's death, which purported to show him, hovering in the background.

Lincoln's ghost has also been seen in Springfield, Illinois, where he was buried. A ghostly train, supposedly Lincoln's funeral cortège, which is black and manned by skeletons, has also been seen steaming its way through the state of Illinois.

FAMOUS GHOSTS

Virginia. It is said that he appears as a young child, full of mischief, who is likely to move objects and ring doorbells. At other times he is seen with a ghostly black dog, accompanied by the spirits of his two sisters.

JESSE JAMES

Jesse Woodson James was born in September 1847. Somewhat inaccurately, he has been labelled a gunfighter, but undoubtedly he was one of America's most famous outlaws.

ROBERT E. LEE

One of Lincoln's famous contemporaries was the Confederate General Robert E. Lee. Through his tactical genius, Lee managed to nurse the Confederacy through innumerable battles against a far more numerous and powerful foe. Ultimately, however, he was forced to surrender at Appomattox Courthouse in April 1865. Unlike many of the other generals in the war, Lee did not meet a violent death, but his spirit can be seen in his childhood home in Alexandria,

OPPOSITE FAR LEFT: Robert E. Lee.

OPPOSITE ABOVE RIGHT: Jessie James.

OPPOSITE BELOW: Appomattox Courthouse, Virginia, where General Lee surrendered to General Ulysses S. Grant.

RIGHT: Jesse James, lying dead in his coffin.

BELOW: Frank James, Jesse's brother.

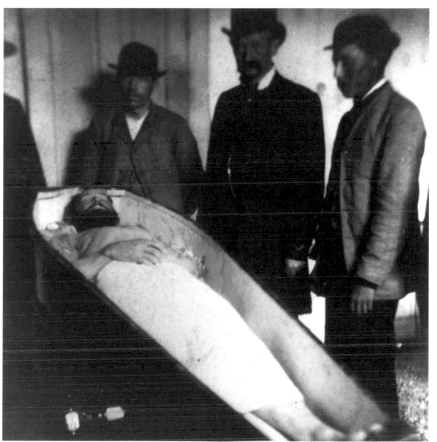

Jesse and his brother Frank were two of Quantrill's Raiders, a guerilla group that terrorized Missouri during the American Civil War.

The James boys were brought up on a farm in Kearney, Missouri, and it is here that Jesse's ghost is sometimes to be seen. The James family was attached to the place, where both joy and tragedy had been experienced. Jesse's mother, Zerelda, had had three husbands and eight children at the farm, but it was also the place where Union militia whipped Jesse James and where he witnessed the hanging of his stepfather. The farm also witnessed the death of Archie Samuel at the hands of Pinkerton detectives, and Zerelda lost her right hand in the same incident.

With a $10,000 bounty on his head, members of his own gang finally shot Jesse James; his body was buried at the farm, although it would be later re-interred at the Mount Olivet Cemetery. Spirits haunt the farmhouse and lights can be seen moving both inside and around it at night. Cries, shots and pounding hooves are also heard, reminiscent of the American Civil War. Despite all this, however, none of the phenomena has ever been recorded on the security cameras.

LIZZIE BORDEN
The Borden house in Fall River, Massachusetts, is now a bed-and-breakfast establishment, but it is where young Lizzie Borden, on 4 August 1892, claimed the lives of her father, Andrew, and stepmother, Abby, in a horrendous and bloody double murder:

> *'Lizzie Borden took an axe*
> *Gave her mother forty whacks*
> *When she saw what she had done*
> *Gave her father forty-one.'*

To this day opinion is divided on the subject of Lizzie Borden and the reason why she murdered her parents. Some

time before the murders, she had apparently practised using an axe by decapitating her own cat.

Although Lizzie was tried for the murders, she was acquitted, and the case continues to be the subject of enormous speculation as a result.

Originally the house had been built for two families in around 1845. Unlike many other scenes of crimes, the building remains intact, and has been in private ownership for decades. There

have been numerous reports of people hearing a woman crying at night, while others have had the chilling experience of a woman tucking them up in bed at night, or have seen their shoes move across the floor.

These occurences seem to be the work of Andrew and Abby, rather than Lizzie Borden; they seem to delight in making the lights flicker and whenever investigators into the paranormal arrive, their recording equipment is switched off and their cameras on.

JEREMY BENTHAM
Jeremy Bentham, an eccentric English philosopher who died in 1832, was the co-founder of University College in Gower Street, London. He always wore a distinctive, broad-brimmed hat and white gloves, and had a walking stick which he called Dapple.

In his will, Bentham requested that his body be used for medical research, and that once it had been dissected,

LEFT: The embalmed body of Jeremy Bentham.

OPPOSITE: University College, London. Jeremy Bentham was a co-founder of the university.

The Anne Frank House, on the Prinsengracht in Amsterdam, is now a museum dedicated to the Jewish wartime diarist Anne Frank.

Anne, in her diaries, referred to the achterhuis, *or back house, as the 'secret annex', which was hidden from view by houses on all four sides. Its secluded position made it an ideal hiding place for Otto Frank, his wife Edith, two daughters (of whom Anne was the youngest), and four other Jewish people seeking refuge from the Nazis during the German occupation of the Netherlands in World War II. Eventually they were all arrested and Anne died of typhus in the Bergen-Belsen concentration camp within days of her sister, Margot. Her father, Otto, the only survivor of the group, returned to Amsterdam after the war ended, to find that her diary had survived.*

Visitors to the secret annex have felt cold spots in certain areas, while Anne's ghost has been seen looking out of her window at the back around midnight. There have also been reports of a loud rumbling sound coming from the basement; this is connected with an event in Anne's life, when a a sack of uncooked beans accidently fell down the stairs.

was to be reassembled and dressed in his own clothes, joined by a wax facsimile of his head. Then he was to be sat in his favourite chair, holding Dapple in his hand, and be placed in a mahogany, glass-sided case, near to the main entrance of the college.

Bentham's ghost has been seen on many occasions, sometimes tapping his stick on the glass front of the case, possibly indicating that he now wishes to have a proper burial. There was a recent sighting by a teacher at the university, who claimed to have seen Bentham's ghost, which turned and walked towards him. Terrified, the teacher expected an imminent collision, but the apparition simply passed straight through him, before disappearing from view.

HARRY PRICE

One of the most famous of the ghost-hunters, Harry Price founded the National Laboratory of Psychical Research at the University of London, and carried out many investigations into the paranormal (see page 40, Borley Rectory). It should come as no great surprise, therefore, that when Price died in March 1948, he would himself return as a ghost.

In life, Price swore that, if it were at all possible, he would come back, but he would not have expected this to have happened in such a dramatic style. Price made his first appearance in Sweden, in the form of an elderly, balding man, standing beside the bed of a young man. The Swede spoke no English, but somehow the apparition was able to communicate the fact to him that his name was Harry Price. The Swede, his wife, and daughter, saw the ghost on a regular basis. He described

it as not as one would imagine a ghost to look, but rather more solid, prompting him to take photographs. When they were developed, however, nothing at all could be seen. The Swede determined to learn English so that, in future, he could converse with Price's ghost.

The ghost warned the man that he was suffering from a serious medical problem, and should see a doctor. As luck would have it, the doctor whom the Swede consulted was interested in psychical research and was in no doubt that the apparition was indeed genuine. To this day, no one can understand why Harry Price, an Englishman, appeared to a non-English-speaking man in another country.

ABOVE LEFT: Harry Price was the most famous of the psychical researchers, his most famouse case being the investigation into the Borley Rectory hauntings.

OPPOSITE: Séances were popular in the 1800s, and those held by the medium Jonathan Coons were no exception. Here a group are attempting to levitate a musical instrument.

THE KING FAMILY

The spirit world of the King family was presented in a well-documented set of cases originating from a log cabin in Athens County, Ohio, in 1852. At the time, Jonathan Coons, supposedly a medium but also something of a showman, owned the cabin. He was probably a fake, which did not prevent him from being immensely popular with the public.

The first to manifest itself at one of Coons's séances was John King, a colourful phantom, who in life had supposedly been a pirate, but by far the most popular member of the King family was Katie. She had also appeared to other mediums, including the Italian Eusapia Palladino and the English Florence Cook. Cook is credited with being the first medium ever to have materialized a spirit in its entire human form, but many dismissed the incident as trickery – as some sort of manipulation with a bed sheet. Nevertheless, photographs were produced and whether they were faked or not is open to conjecture.

Sir William Crookes, although he was a believer in spiritualism himself, was no one's fool. He was also associated with the development of the

X-ray, and was president of The Royal Society, the most important scientific body in the world.

In 1874 an agreement was made with Florence Cook that Sir William would scientifically examine the phenomenon, and to this end, many of the séances were held, under controlled conditions, in Crookes's home. In a séance on 29 March, Crookes and another scientist witnessed Florence Cook, crouching on the floor, with the figure of Katie King standing behind her. Another Royal Society scientist used a phosphorescent lamp to illuminate the figures, and Crookes was able to take a series of photographs over the next few weeks. One of these photographs was of Katie and Florence Cook together, but this, unfortunately has since disappeared.

There would appear to be three explanations of these strange events: either that Katie was indeed a ghost; or that Cook was a fraud and had deceived everyone by her clever manipulations; or that William Crookes himself had been a party in the deception.

THE VOODOO QUEENS

Marie Laveau, the voodoo queen of New Orleans, reputedly haunts the site where 1020 St. Ann Street stands, and is still said to be performing magic from beyond the grave. In the sense that she truly believed in the occult and in her own magic powers, Marie was no charlatan. She was a fervent Roman Catholic, who also brought traditional African magic and ritual into her religious life.

Out of the local history of New Orleans, two Maries emerge: one a free woman of colour, born in New Orleans in the mid 1790s, the other a considerably younger woman, believed to have been Marie Laveau's illegitimate daughter. The two were remarkably similar in appearance, so much so that when the mother died, the daughter assumed her place, the two merging seamlessly into one another to

LEFT: Much of Marie Laveau's magic originally came from Africa. A dried stork is pictured here, on sale in a voodoo market in Lomé, Togo.

OPPOSITE: New Orleans, Louisiana, where Marie Laveau and her daughter lived and cast their magic spells.

give the illusion of a single person blessed with the gift of eternal youth.

By profession, Marie Laveau was a hairdresser, which was how she knew so much about her wealthy clients. She was a feared and respected figure, with a wide knowledge of sorcery and potions of all kinds; but her real power lay in her hold over her many informants, many of whom were servants of her clients, who were too afraid of her not to tell her all they knew.

Marie Laveau's most famous exploit involved the murder trial of a young Creole, destined to end in a guilty verdict. Marie was approached by his wealthy father, who promised her anything she desired to save his son. Marie agreed, demanding the man's New Orleans house in return. He agreed, and Marie planted magic charms throughout the courtroom. When the boy was declared not guilty, Marie got the house, and became even more famous as a result.

Some say Marie was a werewolf, while others claim she changed herself into the black crow, seen flying over the old St. Louis cemetery, where she lay buried in the family crypt. Visitors still visit her grave, and leave petitions and voodoo offerings even to this day.

71

*Knebworth House, Hertfordshire, England.
Sir Robert Lytton bought the house at the
end of the 15th century, gradually
transforming it into a Tudor mansion,
which it largely remained for 300 years.
From the beginning of the 19th century
onwards, various alterations were made by
different members of the family (including
those of Sir Edward Bulwer-Lytton, who
was responsible for the rather eccentric and
fanciful 'Gothic' exterior), until the house
became largely as it appears today.*

*Sir Edward Bulwer-Lytton, the famous
Victorian novelist and playwright, who was
interested in the occult and was linked with
the Order of the Golden Dawn, invited the
famous medium, Daniel Dunglass, to
Knebworth. Here séances were held,
resulting in many strange phenomena.
Edward's ghostly presence has been felt by
many in the house, usually in the study
and the drawing room, although he is yet to
be seen.*

*The sound of a spinning wheel can also
be heard in the house, said to come from a
spirit called Spinning Jenny, who was
locked in her room to prevent her from
meeting her lowly lover. There is also a
story concerning the appearance of a
radiant boy, a spirit associated with the
Lytton family. These spectres are common
in other old families, and Lord Castlereagh
was the last to see one before cutting his
own throat.*

THE WITCH OF ENDOR

This story appears in the Book of Samuel and was written in about 1000 BC. It is one of the strangest and most contradictory episodes recorded in the Bible, since King Saul himself had presumably already banished occult practices from the land of Israel.

Israel was under threat of a Philistine invasion at that time, and having consulted God on the matter and received no reply, King Saul assumed that he had been forsaken. Gripped by fear of what would happen, Saul decided to consult the Witch of Endor.

The Old Testament forbade occult practices of any kind and death was the punishment for anyone found consulting mediums. Saul decided to

RIGHT & OPPOSITE LEFT: Harry Houdini, a man noted for his escape acts.

OPPOSITE CENTRE: A challenge to Houdini to make a particularly difficult escape.

OPPOSITE RIGHT: Sir Arthur Conan Doyle was a close friend of Houdini, who failed to be impressed by Doyle's wife's ability as a medium.

ignore this, and in disguise and under cover of darkness went to Endor to consult the witch, promising she would not be punished if she summoned the Prophet Samuel up from the dead.

The witch agreed, and as she had abandoned her usual trickery, she was genuinely shocked when an old man appeared. What was presumably Samuel's spirit angrily predicted Saul's downfall, told him that Israel would be defeated and that both Saul and his sons would die at the hands of the Philistines.

HOUDINI

Harry Houdini was a Hungarian whose real name was Erik Weisz. He was not only a famous escapologist, but also a man who doubted the claims of spiritualists. As nearly everyone knows, Houdini died from peritonitis, resulting

mother, and desperately tried to communicate with her. He enlisted the support of a close friend, Sir Arthur Conan Doyle, whose wife was an amateur medium, and it was during one of these séances that Houdini reached the conclusion that all spiritualists were charlatans.

Doyle's wife made contact with Houdini's dead mother and received a message in English from her for her son. Unfortunately she had never been able to speak or write in English, making Houdini aware that this was a fake.

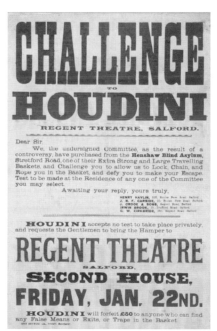

from a ruptured appendix, at Halloween, in 1926.

Houdini had been drawn to spiritualism after the death of his

So that he would be able to test mediums for himself after his death, Houdini prepared a special code, known only to himself and to his wife, Beatrice. This was so that any message, purporting to have come from Houdini, could be immediately identified if it were false. After Houdini's death, Beatrice received dozens of spurious messages from her husband via various mediums around the world. Then, in 1928, she received one through an American medium called Arthur Ford.

Rumour has it, however, that Beatrice, having confirmed Ford's claims that he had indeed made contact with her late husband, had actually conspired with Ford in order to make money from a lecture tour. For the rest of her life, however, she persistantly denied that any conspiracy had taken place. Somewhat bizarrely, there are mediums around the world who, to this day claim to have contacted Harry Houdini's spirit, though the truth of the matter may never be known.

BONNIE AND CLYDE

Bonnie Parker and Clyde Barrow, dubbed the Romeo and Juliet of crime, were notorious criminals, who operated during America's Great Depression. They met in Texas in January 1930, when Clyde had already been in and out of jail for burglary and car theft. At the time, Bonnie was 19 and married to an imprisoned murderer, and Clyde was 21 and unmarried. Soon afterwards, Clyde was arrested for a burglary and was sent to jail. He escaped, using a gun Bonnie had smuggled into prison for him, was recaptured, and was returned to prison. Clyde rejoined Bonnie when he was paroled in February 1932, and together they resumed their life of crime, committing even more nefarious deeds.

Barrow came to be suspected of numerous killings and was wanted for

murder, robbery, and kidnap. The pair were shot to death in a police ambush near Sailes, Louisiana, on 23 May 1934, after one of the most spectacular manhunts America had experienced up to that time.

Afterwards, their bullet-ridden car was towed into town. Beside the road, where they had fallen beneath the hail of bullets, the spot is marked. This marker is often photographed, and ghostly forms can sometimes be seen lurking in the background.

RUDOLPH VALENTINO

On 6 May 1895 Rodolfo Alfonso Raffaello Piero Filiberto Guglielmi was born in Italy. He arrived in New York on Christmas Day when he was 18 years old. No one could have known then that under the name of Rudolph Valentino, this waiter and gardener would become one of the great icons of the American cinema.

After starring in some of the most romantic silent movies ever made in Hollywood, Valentino's career was

OPPOSITE: Bonnie Parker pretending to shoot Clyde Barrow.

ABOVE: Rudolph Valentino.

LEFT: The bullet-ridden car in which the infamous Bonnie and Clyde were killed. They were shot by police near their Louisiana hide-out on 23 May 1934.

tragically cut short in August 1926, when he collapsed at the Hotel Ambassador in New York City and was rushed to hospital with a perforated ulcer. Peritonitis unfortunately set in, and eight days later the 'Latin lover' was dead at the age of 31.

Around 100,000 people attended his funeral, but it is a macabre fact that the body, placed on view at the funeral home, was only a wax effigy of the star.

Valentino's ghost is said to have become active shortly after his death, appearing most often at his former mansion in Hollywood, the Falcon's Lair, where he would be seen peering out of a window on the second floor. Others have seen him in the hallways, and a stable lad was so spooked at

LEFT: The Ambassador Hotel, now re-named, where Rudolph Valentino collapsed with a perforated ulcer, dying eight days later at the age of 31.

OPPOSITE LEFT: At one time, Pola Negri was believed to be the Lady in Black who haunted Valentino's grave.

OPPOSITE RIGHT: Forest Lawn Memorial Park, where the body of Lon Chaney rests in an unmarked crypt.

seeing Valentino in the stables, stroking his favourite horse, that he fled the mansion never to return. Valentino has also been sighted in the Santa Maria Inn, where he reclines on a bed and knocks on doors. Dressed as a sheik, a character from two of his most popular movies, he has also been seen in the costume department at Paramount Studios, above Studio 5, while others have seen him at his former beach

house at Oxnard, Ventura County, California.

Valentino's Great Dane, Kabar, outlived his master by three years and its ghost is said to wander the Los Angeles Pet Cemetery. Another sighting related to Valentino is that of a Lady in Black, who has been spotted in the vicinity of Crypt 1205 in Hollywood's Memorial Cathedral Mausoleum. For several years this was thought to be the Polish actress, Pola Negri, although she did not die until 1987. Whoever she was in life or death, the Black Lady can sometimes be seen laying flowers on Valentino's grave.

LON CHANEY

Coming a close second to Valentino, in terms of frequent sightings, is the ghost of Lon Chaney Sr. He was known as the 'man of a thousand faces', so it is hardly surprising that, after he died in 1930, he should be seen in so many different locations. Chaney developed pneumonia in the winter of 1929 and was to die the following year of a throat hemorrhage caused by cancer. His crypt in the Forest Lawn Memorial Park Cemetery in Glendale, California, is unmarked.

His favourite haunt was a bench at the corner of Hollywood and Vine, close to the bus stop. This was where he used to wait in life, when working as an extra in the early years. Even after he became famous, he still drove past the bench, looking for other aspiring actors who could be used as extras. After his death it became something of a tradition that no one else should sit on the bench, since it was reserved for Chaney's ghost, but all sightings of him ceased when the bench was removed in 1942.

Chaney's spirit still frequents sound stage 28 at Universal Studios, where true to form, having appeared in the Phantom of the Opera in 1925, he appears in the same guise. He is also thought to be responsible for lights that turn on and off around the set, and doors that open and close of their own accord.

JEAN HARLOW

Jean Harlow was born in 1911 and despite having had a short acting career in the 1930s, she became the archetypal sex symbol and blonde bombshell. She was the daughter of a dentist from Missouri and would star opposite Clark Gable and Spencer Tracy.

In 1932 Harlow's second husband, Paul Bern, an MGM producer, was

OPPOSITE: Jean Harlow, the archetypal blonde bombshell, died tragically at the age of 26. Her ghost is also said to haunt Glendale's Forest Lawn Memorial Park.

LEFT: Although Clark Gable remarried twice after the death of Carole Lombard in 1933, he was buried beside her after he died in 1960.

found dead at their home, leading to scandal and speculation as to why he should have killed himself. It was rumoured that he was actually murdered by Dorothy Millette, who supposedly committed suicide the following day. The chill of death seems to have remained in the house, as Sharon Tate would later own the property; she was murdered there in August 1969 by followers of the notorious Charles Manson.

MGM tried to hush up the scandal of Paul Bern's death, as by this stage, Harlow was one of its biggest stars. In 1937, when she was starring opposite Clark Gable in *Saratoga*, Harlow collapsed with kidney failure, which some attribute to a childhood illness, exacerbated by being beaten by her husband. Her then-lover, William Powell, remained by her bedside, but she died a few days later at the age of 26. She, too, was buried at the Forest Lawn Memorial Park in Glendale.

Harlow's ghost, together with that of Paul Bern, has been seen on many occasions at the mansion that they once both occupied in life.

CAROLE LOMBARD

Carole Lombard was born Jane Alice Peters in Indiana in 1908, destined to become the top comedy actress of the 1930s and to marry Clark Gable in 1939. Their married life was reputed to be idyllic and they were to buy a ranch together in California's San Fernando Valley.

At 0400 on 16 January 1942, Lombard and her mother, having appeared at a War Bond Rally, boarded an aircraft in Indiana to make the return

RIGHT: Carole Lombard married Clark Gable in 1939. Their ghosts are said to haunt the Oatman Hotel in Arizona, where they spent their honeymoon.

OPPOSITE: Al Capone was the leader of a crime syndicate in Chicago during the Prohibition era in America. His ghost is said to appear when anyone is disrespectful to the family burial plot.

flight to California. A stop for refuelling was made at Las Vegas and 23 minutes later the aircraft struck Mount Potosi, killing everyone on board.

Lombard was only 33 at the time and Gable was so distraught that he joined the American Air Force, and flew combat missions over Europe. He died in 1960, and even though he had remarried twice since her death, he was buried alongside Lombard. Their ghosts can be seen at the Oatman Hotel in Oatman, Arizona, where the couple had spent their honeymoon.

AL CAPONE

The son of a barber from Naples in Italy, Al Capone was born in Brooklyn, New York in 1899, and was the leader of a crime syndicate in Chicago during the Prohibition era of the 1920s and '30s. The authorities were unable to pin any particular crime on Capone, however, and pursued him for tax evasion instead. He remained a power to be reckoned with, even after he had been imprisoned in Alcatraz in San Francisco Bay. Capone eventually began to deteriorate, suffering a stoke on 21 January 1947. He subsequently caught pneumonia and died of a heart attack a few days later.

LEFT & ABOVE: Al Capone was imprisoned in Alcatraz for tax evasion, and died there eventually of a heart attack.

OPPOSITE: The White Horse Tavern in Greenwich Village, where the poet Dylan Thomas liked to drink, sending himself to an early grave

Although Capone was at first buried in Mount Olivet Cemetery, Chicago, alongside the graves of his father and brother, all three bodies were moved in 1950 to Mount Carmel Cemetery, in Hillside. His ghost is said to appear if anyone visiting the graves shows disrespect. Curators of the former prison on Alcatraz, as well as visitors, have also heard and seen things related to Capone; he was one of the prison's first inmates and banjo music can be heard coming from his cell.

DYLAN THOMAS

Dylan Thomas was born in Swansea, Wales, in 1914. He was a celebrated poet and writer, but met his end at the White Horse Tavern in Greenwich Village, Manhattan. Thomas was a notoriously heavy drinker and on the fateful day had drunk at least 18 shots of whisky, after which he returned to the Chelsea Hotel in New York, whence he was taken to St. Vincent's Hospital. He contracted pneumonia, which caused pressure on the brain, and the effects of alcohol on his liver was a contributing factor to his death on 9 November 1953.

Even though his body was returned to Wales for burial, his ghost seems to

have preferred his favourite corner table at the White Horse Tavern.

JAMES DEAN
Although he died more than 50 years ago, James Dean still retains his iconic status as a rebellious youth. His ghost has not been seen, but his Porsche Spyder was undoubtedly the love of his life, and it was in this car that he died near Cholame, California, on 30 September 1955. Shortly after he had

ABOVE: The interior of the White Horse Tavern has changed very little since Dylan Thomas's time.

OPPOSITE: The Welsh poet and writer, Dylan Thomas.

taken delivery of the car, he showed it to the British actor, Alec Guinness who, it appears, seems to have had a bad feeling about the car and advised Dean not to drive it, fearing he would be dead within a week. Dean ignored this advice and was killed. Afterwards the vehicle changed hands several times, and brought injury or death to each successive owner.

MARILYN MONROE

The legendary actress slipped into a coma on 4 August 1962 from which she never awoke. Monroe was just 36 years old and her death is still surrounded by mystery. Her ghost has been seen in at least two locations: in the Hollywood Roosevelt Hotel, where she often used to stay, and where her ghostly image has been seen in the full-length mirror, that

BELOW: Marilyn Monroe with her husband, Arthur Miller. Laurence Olivier, who co-starred with her in The Prince and the Showgirl *(1957), can be seen in the background on the left.*

OPPOSITE: The ghost of Montgomery Clift reputedly haunts room 928 of the Hollywood Roosevelt Hotel.

once hung in her poolside suite, and is now in the hotel lobby; and in the vicinity of her tomb at the Westwood Memorial Cemetery in Los Angeles. There have also been unconfirmed reports that she haunts her Brentwood home, the place where she died; she seems to be saying that her death was not suicide, but the result of an accident.

MONTGOMERY CLIFT

Room 928 of the Hollywood Roosevelt Hotel is haunted by the four-times Oscar-nominated actor, Montgomery Clift. Strange noises are from time to time heard in the room, which has definite cold spots, and the phone is often knocked off its hook, while some guests have felt an invisible hand resting on their shoulder.

Clift used the room for three months in 1953, while he learned his lines for the film, *From Here to Eternity.* He died in 1966, aged 45.

ELVIS PRESLEY

It is hardly surprising that the ghost of Elvis should appear at both Graceland and in the lobby of the Heartbreak Hotel. Presley died in 1977 and what is surprising is that his ghost can be seen getting married to Marilyn Monroe in

the chapel at Graceland, and a similar haunting is repeated in the chapel of the Heartbreak Hotel, across from Graceland in Memphis, where music, said to be 'Diamonds are a Girl's Best Friend', can be heard.

Elvis's ghost has also been seen by a number of stagehands at the Las Vegas Hilton – also in a building once used as RCA's Nashville recording studios in Music Row, which was where some of Elvis's earliest recordings were made.

OPPOSITE: Graceland, Elvis Presley's former home in Memphis, Tennessee.

BELOW: The graves of Presley family members at Graceland.

ORSON WELLES

(George) Orson Welles was born in Wisconsin in 1915, and became one of Hollywood's greatest actors, producers, writers and directors. He died of a heart attack at the age of 70 on 10 October 1985, on the same day that Yul Brynner also died. The ghost of Orson Welles has been sighted at Sweet Lady Jane's restaurant on Melrose Avenue in Los Angeles. This was his favourite restaurant and his caped figure can be seen sitting at his usual table; some have also smelled brandy and cigars.

LIBERACE

One of Wisconsin's even more flamboyant sons, Liberace was of Polish-Italian descent and was one of twins, the other having died at birth. He gave a last live performance on 2 November 1985 at the Radio City Music Hall in New York City, and thereafter steadfastly denied that he was ill. In fact, he was HIV positive and was also suffering from emphysema and heart and liver problems. Liberace died at the age of 67 on 4 February 1987 at his winter residence at Palm Springs, California.

His ghost is said to haunt Carluccio's Tivoli Gardens Restaurant

in Las Vegas, which was designed by Liberace himself and stands next to the Liberace Museum. Here Liberace had his own private lounge and his ghost sometimes appears in the dining room, emerging from the place where the lounge used to be. Unexplained electrical surges have been experienced in the building, doors lock and unlock themselves, and bottles are tipped over.

On one particular day, the electricity supply disconnected itself and all attempts to reconnect it failed. Then someone realized that it was Liberace's birthday and after he had been wished many happy returns, the electricity came back on.

OPPOSITE: Orson Welles, one of Hollywood's greatest actors, writers and directors.

RIGHT: Liberace, wearing one of many of his flamboyant suits.

CHAPTER THREE
HAUNTED PLACES

*B*ecause ghosts are presumed to be manifestations of the dead, it follows that it would be difficult for them to abandon a location that had been important to them in life. In other words, ghosts appear to retain emotional attachments for certain places or situations, that can survive death itself.

FLIGHT 401

This is illustrated by the story of Flight 401, when the TriStar crashed into the Florida Everglades on 29 December 1972. There were 101 fatalities, and two survivors died later on. The Lockheed jetliner was only four months old, and was being flown by an experienced pilot on a routine flight. After the crash, the airline was able to salvage elements of the crashed aircraft and parts were used in other Lockheed TriStars.

Not long after the crash, the ghosts of Bob Loft and Don Repo, the pilot and flight engineer, who had also died in the crash, were seen on numerous occasions by crew members on other Eastern Tri-Stars, especially on the planes that had been fitted with parts salvaged from Flight 401's wreckage. It would appear that Loft and Repo had assumed a protective role, and that even after their deaths had lost none of their concern for passengers and crew.

LEFT: The Everglades, Florida. When Flight 401 crashed here in December 1972, parts of the plane were recovered and used in other Lockheed planes. These retained certain memories connected with the first.

OPPOSITE: A whirlpool on the Niagara river. Niagara has several ghostly tales in its repertoire.

THE OLD ANGEL INN, NIAGARA-ON-THE-LAKE, ONTARIO

During the War of 1812, fought between the United States of America and Great Britain and its colonies (Canada in particular), Captain Swayze, a British soldier, took refuge in the cellars of the Angel Inn. Surprised by American soldiers, Swayze hid in a wine barrel, but was killed by a thrust from a bayonet. During the American retreat, the Inn was burned to the ground, but was rebuilt in 1815.

From the 1820s onwards, various hauntings were reported, including the sounds of footsteps and male laughter coming from the dining room, along with fife and drum music in an upstairs bedroom.

There were apparitions of well-dressed ladies and gentlemen, along with a red-coated man, usually seen in the mirror of the ladies' room, that was located next to the cellar where Swayze met his end.

FORT ERIE, ONTARIO

Fort Erie was the first British fort to be constructed after the French and Indian War was concluded by the Treaty of Paris in 1763. It is located on the southern edge of the town of Fort Erie, across the Niagara river from Buffalo, New York. The fort itself is associated with particularly unpleasant apparitions, including those of a headless man and a man with missing hands.

During the War of 1812, an American sergeant was being shaved with a cut-throat razor by his corporal. Suddenly, a British cannonball struck the fort, leaving the man doing the shaving minus his hands and the other without a head. The story was confirmed during later excavations at the fort, when the body of a headless man, together with a handless arm, were discovered.

THE SCREAMING TUNNEL, NIAGARA FALLS

Before leaving Canada, there is the strange case of a place close to Niagara Falls to report, known as the Screaming Tunnel. It was originally intended as a rail tunnel, but the Grand Trunk Railroad went bankrupt after the First World War, and although the tunnel was finished in time, the tracks were never laid down. Rumour has it that one day an old farmhouse to the south of the tunnel became engulfed in flames. A young girl fled from the building, her clothes on fire, and ran towards the tunnel, throwing herself on the ground in an attempt to extinguish the flames.

The other version of the story is that, after a quarrel concerning her parents' divorce, her father set the girl on fire while in the tunnel; since then, anyone striking a match will hear piercing screams until the match is extinguished.

PORT ARTHUR, TASMANIA, AUSTRALIA

Port Arthur was established in 1830 as a timber station, but a few years later, because it was situated on an isthmus, surrounded by the sea and with restricted access by land, it was turned into a prison settlement where the worst of the convicts that had been transported from Britain were thrown, sentenced to work in chain gangs. Here, much of the timber used to build Sydney was produced.

Over its 47-year history, the place gained a reputation for its harsh regime, where floggings were

OPPOSITE: The Port Arthur prison settlement, Tasmania.

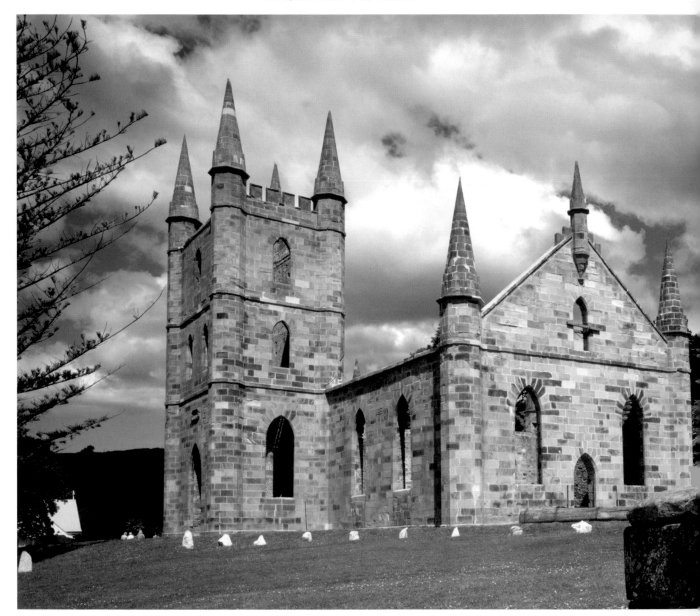

FAR LEFT: Port Arthur's church was built by convicts and was possible never consecrated.

LEFT: Port Arthur's mental hospital.

BELOW: The prison cells.

administered as a matter of course. It finally closed in 1877 and at some point over the next 20 years, fire and theft destroyed most of the buildings. To this day, however, voices can be heard and odd, ghostly manifestations have been witnessed. These are almost certainly related to the men that were condemned to live and work in this grim settlement.

Close by is a church, built between 1836 and 1837, although it is possible that it was never consecrated. During its construction, two men had a fight and one fell to his death from the bell tower. His head struck the outside wall of the church and to this day, although ivy covers most of the ruins, it refuses to grow on that spot. Many have also heard the sound of a ghostly choir, coming from inside the ruins, while others claim to have seen balls of light.

BRISBANE, QUEENSLAND, AUSTRALIA

Brisbane is said to be the most haunted city in Australia. The second floor of the beautifully restored Brisbane Arcade consists of a cast-iron balcony that runs around the walls of the building, but with the centre cut out to

BELOW & OPPOSITE: Brisbane, said to be Australia's most haunted city.

reveal a view of the first floor. It is said that the ghost of a shopkeeper still walks the arcade on the second level, and has been seen by security guards on many occasions.

Brisbane City Hall has three ghosts: one is said to be a workman, who was killed in the 1930s while installing the elevator, and terrifyingly, sometimes joins live passengers for a ride. In the tearoom there is the ghost of an American sailor, who was killed by a fellow rating in a brawl over an Australian girl. People have heard arguing, a knife being drawn, and the sailor gurgling his last breath. Finally, a lady dressed in period costume is often seen standing on the main staircase; she appears to be waiting for someone who never comes.

EDINBURGH, SCOTLAND

Scotland, being an ancient land with a long and eventful history, fairly bristles with 'ghosts and ghoolies ... and things than go bump in the night'. Edinburgh, Scotland's capital city, is a particular hotspot. Outside the city is a rocky, ancient volcanic outcrop, known as Arthur's Seat, reputed to be the resting place of a passing giant. Besides giving extensive views across the Firth of Forth to Fife and the Lomond Hills, many of Edinburgh's famous landmarks can be seen stretched out below.

In 1836, schoolboys found 17 small wooden coffins, each containing a carved figure, in a small cave below the summit. Their existence has never been satisfactorily explained, but links with witchcraft have been suggested. Alternatively, they may be memorials to the victims of the so-called 'Resurrectionists', the name by which the infamous body-snatchers, Burke and Hare, were also known.

Edinburgh's Calton Hill, with its replica Athenian acropolis outlined

against the sky, is where the pagan ritual of Beltane is performed each year, to welcome in the approach of summer. Nearby, there is said to be a portal, leading to the fairy kingdom, which can only be seen by people with the gift of second sight.

Lord Balcarres saw Viscount Dundee in Edinburgh Castle in 1689, when it would have been presumably impossible, since he had just died at the Battle of Killiecrankie, while other phantasmagoria include: Mary, Queen

LEFT: Edinburgh's network of underground passages and ancient buildings make it a 'hot spot' for ghostly sightings.

BELOW: Calton Hill, where the pagan festival of Beltane is still observed.

of Scots, said to haunt Holyrood House; a woman in white, who appears at the Royal Circus Hotel; a tiny girl, reputed to haunt the Sheep's Heid – the oldest public house in Edinburgh; and the naked Lady Hamilton of

The processional stretch of Edinburgh's Royal Mile leads eventually to the magnificent Palace of Holyrood House, built by order of James IV in 1498, though little of the original building is left today. The most famous marriage to take place here was that of the 22-year-old Mary, Queen of Scots to the 19-year-old Darnley, on 29 July 1565. It turned out to be an unhappy and tragic marriage, as did her marriage to the Earl of Bothwell on 15 May 1567. Given her turbulent life, therefore, it is little wonder that Mary's ghost is said to wander the palace.

The majestic ruins of Whitby Abbey, in North Yorkshire, England. First established in AD 657 on a cliff overlooking the sea, the Benedictine abbey, for both men and women, was destroyed by the Vikings some 200 years later, then rebuilt by the conquering Normans in 1067.

Hilda, the niece of the King of Northumbria, was its first abbess and she apparently never left the site. Her ghost, wrapped in a shroud, frequently appears at one of the abbey's highest windows. During her tenure at Whitby, she was noted for ridding the area of snakes, driving them to the cliff's edge where she decapitated them with a whip. Possibly connected with this story is another of a great hearse-like coach, guided by a headless driver and pulled by four headless horses, which has been seen racing along the cliff before plunging over the edge and into the sea.

But a rather more troubled ghost is that of Constance de Beverley, a young nun, who broke her vows for the love of a brave but false knight named Marmion. Her punishment was to be bricked up alive in a dungeon in the abbey. Her ghost has been seen on the winding stairway leading from the dungeon, where she cowers, begging for release.

Captain James Cook has associations with the town of Whitby, and its churchyard inspired Bram Stoker's novel, Dracula.

FAR RIGHT: Wawel Castle. John Dee, the English alchemist and magician, visited Krakow in 1584, in search of spirits.

Bothwellhaugh, who wanders in the ruins of Woodhouse Lee. It is said that Lady Hamilton was banished into the night when her husband's castle was taken. She was thrown out without a stitch on her back and eventually froze to death. Her naked ghost has been seen in the area, sometimes holding the body of her dead child.

KRAKOW, POLAND

Krakow, a city associated with clay monsters, dragons and the horrors of the Second World War, seems to have spirits literally springing from its ancient stones. Many of the stories are connected with Wawel Castle, a magnificent structure, situated atop Wawel Hill, and said to be the spiritual heart of Poland. Many of the old kings of Poland were crowned here and lie buried in the castle vaults.

Many have heard eerie music coming from the vaults, while others have complained of feeling heavy and oppressed. The hill itself is riddled with caves; inside is the Dragon's Lair, where there is a statue of a dragon, probably in honour of a pagan serpent goddess, said to have lived inside the hill.

The court jester, Stanczyk, formerly of the court of King Sigismund, is said to appear on the battlements of the castle whenever Poland is in danger, having been a fanatical Polish patriot during his lifetime.

The building that is currently the mayor's office was once a magnificent mansion, said to be haunted by a young woman, called Miss Wielopolski. She fell in love with a poor man and her father, rather than allowing her to bring shame upon the family, decided to murder his daughter. Being a devout man, he first blindfolded and kidnapped a young priest from St Mary's Church, bringing him to hear his daughter's confession before he carried out the deed. She made her confession, then an executioner appeared and sliced off her head.

The father gave the executioner and the priest a drink: the executioner drank his, but the priest poured his drink down his clerical collar. He was blindfolded again, before being taken away. When he arrived home, the priest saw that the skin of his neck and chest had blistered and realized that an attempt had been made to poison him.

Many years later, the priest had cause to visit the house, not recognizing it as the place where he had heard the girl's confession until he had passed through the door. Immediately, he turned the father in to the authorities, who was executed for ordering his own daughter's murder. The girl still haunts the building.

In the 19th century, some nuns built a shrine outside the high walls of the Carmelite convent on Kopernika Street, either as an act of contrition for treating one of their fellows badly, or to give thanks that they had escaped being found out. Legend has it that the victim was a nun who had eloped with her lover, but who had been caught and brought back to the convent. As punishment, she was walled up in a tiny room for the rest of her life. Her ghost has also been seen on the street and, rather alarmingly, walking through the high walls.

PRAGUE

For many, the city of Prague, now in the Czech Republic, is all about its magnificent castle and cathedral, but it is the Charles Bridge that holds a terrifying and eerie secret. For many years during the Middle Ages, the

LEFT: Wawel Cathedral. Wawel Hill is riddled with underground caves, and a legend of King Kazimierz the Great tells how, as a boy, he found his way into the hill and into a chamber, lit by the warm glow of a mysterious stone, said to be the source of the mystic energy pervading Krakow.

OPPOSITE: Prague, showing St. Vitus's Cathedral, the Castle and the Charles Bridge.

heads of people executed in the city were stuck onto poles, and exhibited on the bridge for all to see. Many people are reputed to have heard the heads, still on their poles, singing around the midnight hour. On the bridge is a statue of Prince Bruncvik, and inside it is reputed to be a magic sword, that could be ordered to cut off heads. It is unwise to swim too near to the bridge, not only because the strong current of the River Vltava carries one away, but also because a water goblin hides within its depths, waiting to devour the souls of the drowned.

The Thirty Years War raged in Europe between 1618 and 1648, pitting Protestants against Catholics and bringing famine, disease and death. The Protestant Swedes captured Prague

OPPOSITE: The Charles Bridge links Old Prague with the Malá Strana and Prague Castle.

RIGHT: St. Vitus's Cathedral towers above a city full of folklore and legend.

during the war and one of their slain soldiers can be seen riding his horse along the streets – headless, and carrying his own head in a sack beneath his arm.

A rather portly ghost also frequents the area, condemned to wander after his death because of his refusal to share his food with starving beggars.

Prague's old Jewish quarter is at the centre of the famous story of the Golem, created by the Rabbi Loew in the 16th century to protect the Jewish population from pogroms. According to the Kabbala, a Golem could be made from clay taken from the banks of the Vltava. Following the prescribed rituals, the Rabbi brought the giant to life by pressing the word *emet*, meaning 'truth', on the Golem's forehead. The Golem obeyed the Rabbi at first, but as it grew it became increasingly out of control. There was nothing for it but to destroy the Golem, and the Rabbi accomplished this by changing the

The ruins of the 12th-century Bolton Abbey, near Skipton, Yorkshire, stand on the banks of the River Wharfe, surrounded by fields. Founded in 1151 by Augustinian monks, the remains and its setting have been immortalized both in art and poetry – in a painting by Edwin Landseer and in watercolours by J.M.W. Turner, one of which, Bolton Abbey, Yorkshire (1809), is in the British Museum. William Wordsworth's poem, 'The White Doe of Rylstone', was inspired by a visit to Bolton Abbey in 1807.

The Marquis of Hartington saw the ghost of a monk in the rectory in 1912, while in 1975 the Reverend F.G. Griffiths confirmed that the apparition of an Augustinian friar was seen walking through the wall of the rectory towards the ruined abbey. This figure has also been witnessed by visitors to the ruins on a number of occasions. A black-robed spectre is also said to haunt the site, usually during daylight hours in the month of July, when it is accompanied by a powerful smell of incense.

word *emet* to *met*, meaning 'death', and the Golem accordingly died. According to legend, the Golem was brought back to life by Rabbi Loew's son, and may still be protecting Prague to this day.

BERLIN, GERMANY

The royal architect, Caspar Theiss, designed and built a hunting lodge for his patron, Elector Prince Joachim II in the 1540s, hidden away in dense forest near the Grunewald lake, now a municipal district of Berlin. The place is allegedly haunted by the ghost of a Prussian nobleman, who was murdered by one of the Hohenzollern princes in a fit of rage. The prince chased the nobleman down a staircase, leading from the upper storey to the ground floor, and eventually caught him up.

The staircase was bricked up, but the sounds of someone running down the stairs can be clearly heard. Over the decades, attempts have been made to tear the wall down, but permission has always been refused. Perhaps the remains of the victim are still lying at the bottom of the flight of stairs.

The original Berlin Castle was built in 1443 and for nearly 200 years was the main residence of the kings of Prussia and the emperors of Germany.

When the German monarchy fell in 1918, Burg Hohenzollern became a museum, but was severely damaged by Allied bombing during the Second World War, causing it to be demolished in 1950.

Legend has it that a White Lady (*Weisse Frau*), identified as Kunigunde von Orlamonde, whose family built the castle, murdered her two children by piercing their skulls with a golden needle. Her troubled conscience took her to Rome to see the Pope, who told her she would be forgiven if she spent the rest of her life in a monastery. She established her own monastery, but nonetheless still haunts all of the Hohenzollern castles, foretelling death and bringing bad luck to those passing through her shadow.

THE PARIS CATACOMBS, FRANCE

Beneath the streets of Paris lay the skeletons of seven million disinterred Parisians, stacked neatly along the passageways. The Paris catacombs were originally stone quarries, and over the years, as the cemeteries filled up, older bones were moved underground. The catacombs are said to emanate an eerie, blue mist, that seems to create swirling

BELOW & OPPOSITE LEFT: King Louis XIV. Louis made Versailles the virtual capital of France during his reign.

OPPOSITE RIGHT: Versailles is also famous for the ghostly phenomena connected with the place.

the Black Death and the slaughter of the Hundred Years' War (1337–1453). It comes as no great surprise, therefore, that the area is very haunted.

Back in 1901, a couple of English spinsters were visiting Versailles for the first time. As they approached the palace they saw a woman shaking a

forms that change direction, creating strange apparitions and shapes; some say they smell of sandalwood.

THE GHOSTS OF VERSAILLES

The Palais de Versailles is probably the most visited building in France. It is closely associated with King Louis XIV, who made it the unofficial capital of France in the late 17th century.

There may well have been an abbey on the site as early as 1038 and a small castle and a church in later years. The village itself was virtually wiped out by

cloth out of a window. Then, as they turned a corner, a farm came into view. The labourers they met were wearing peculiar clothes and tricorn hats, and a man ran up to them and spoke to them in an odd accent. The women took in the bucolic scene for some moments, then resumed walking until the palace came into view in all its glory. What had happened was that they had moved back to a past time dimension, then forward, returning to the present.

These two ladies were not the only ones to experience this odd phenomenon. In 1932 a teacher and pupil saw a woman and an old man wearing 18th-century clothes. They tried to speak to the man but failed to understand the way he spoke French.

In 1949 a poultry farmer from England clearly saw a woman dressed in old-fashioned clothing. His wife also saw her and after they had looked at illustrations of clothing from the period, they were certain that it was from around 1870. A London solicitor and his wife saw a woman, wearing a very bright dress, walking with two men on 21 May 1955. They approached them, but the trio immediately vanished before their eyes.

Venice at night, with its dark passages and waterways, is not only beautiful but also eerie. There are many ghost stories associated with the area, including those of Castle Brando and Count Brandolini.

CASTLE BRANDO, NR. VENICE, ITALY

Over the years, Castelbrando, located in Cison di Valmarino, has been visited by Dante Alighieri, Vivaldi and Casanova, but legends of apparitions seen at the castle all seem to emanate from Count Brandolini, who in his lifetime was a feared and hated man.

Brandolini always exercised his *droit de seigneur*, and the brides of his vassals were required to spend their wedding night, not with their husbands, but with the count. Any women who rejected the count's advances were beheaded, their bodies cast through a trapdoor in the count's bedroom. It is said that screaming heads were once seen rolling down the mountainside, and their cries can be heard to this day. The trapdoor was still in existence during the First World War, when it was used as an escape route out of the castle.

The Abbey of Mont-Saint-Michel sits high upon a rocky island, lying between Normandy and Brittany in France, in the midst of vast sandbanks that are exposed to powerful tides.

In 708, a dream inspired St.-Aubert, the Bishop of Avranches, to create a shrine to the Archangel Michael on this site. In 966, the Duke of Normandy entrusted the sanctuary to the care of Benedictine friars, who proceeded to build a magnificent abbey on the site, that would become one of the major destinations of medieval pilgrimage in Europe.

Many ghost stories are connected with the site, its most famous spectre being that of Louis d'Estouville, the commander of the garrison there in 1434, who successfully defended the abbey from a powerful English army. It is said that the blood of 2,000 Englishmen turned the sand red, and that d'Estouville's ghost is destined to haunt Mont-Saint-Michel for eternity.

When the old London Bridge, built in 1831, began to find London's ever-increasing traffic difficult to support, it was moved to Lake Havasu City. It seems, however, that some of the bridge's English ghosts were loath to leave the bridge, and came to Arizona for the ride.

It is said that the count still haunts the castle grounds; his ghost has been seen, riding a horse, supposedly searching for his lost soul.

LONDON BRIDGE, RE-ERECTED IN ARIZONA
Jack Williams, the Governor of Arizona, and Sir Peter Studd, the Lord Mayor of London, officially opened London Bridge at Lake Havasu City in Arizona in October 1971. The old bridge, in what could be described as a monumental dismantling and reconstruction exercise, had been brought from London and transported across the Atlantic Ocean to its new home. But it seems that the physical

LEFT: Manhattan's earliest ghostly sighting was around 1799, when the ghost of Peter Stuyvesant was seen at St. Mark's Church (see overleaf).

BELOW: Dutch soldiers, led by Peter Stuyvesant, leaving Niew Amsterdam after ceding it to the English.

The earliest sighting in the area probably dates from around 1799, when the ghost of one of the city's most influential mayors, Peter Stuyvesant, was supposedly seen. This occurred in St. Mark's Church, that stands on East 10th

components of the bridge were not the only things to have been brought; ghosts wearing Victorian dress also decided to come along for the ride.

MANHATTAN, NEW YORK CITY

The New York borough of Manhattan, being the commercial, financial and cultural centre of New York City, retains many famous architectural landmarks and attractions. The name Manhattan is derived from *manna-hata*, meaning 'island of many hills' in the Native American Delaware language.

Street, between Union Square and Astor Place, where he appeared complete with his wooden leg.

Chumley's, on Bedford Street, was a former speakeasy, and there is still no sign outside. It was also a popular meeting-place of the intelligentsia, including Steinbeck, Scott Fitzgerald, Eugene O'Neill, Dos Passos, Faulkner, Anaïs Nin, Orson Welles, Edna St. Vincent Millay and James Thurber. It is now a popular bar and restaurant, hidden behind a residential block. The original owner, Henrietta Chumley, is said to haunt the building. Seemingly, she is in the habit of moving furniture around when no one is looking.

The Bronx used to have an old hospital that was pulled down in the 1830s, so that Fordham University could be built. Some of the buildings stand on the site of the old mortuary and crematorium, and the area is heavily haunted. There have been a number of ghostly sightings, and chairs are moved and doors opened and closed, apparently without live intervention.

ALCATRAZ, SAN FRANCISCO, CALIFORNIA

Alcatraz, a rocky island in the middle

OPPOSITE & LEFT: St. Mark's Church, New York City.

PAGE 126: The prison on Alcatraz came to be haunted by many notorious characters, including Al Capone.

of San Francisco Bay, used to be called the 'island of the pelicans', and Native Americans held the belief that the island was the home of evil spirits, and avoided it accordingly. But it was during Alcatraz's time as a federal prison that the location became not only infamous, but also the abode of several ghosts.

Al Capone not only died in the prison, but also returned to haunt it, and others of his contemporaries are reputed to visit the place to this day. They include such spectres as George 'Machine-gun' Kelly, who is seen in the prison's church and in the laundry, and Alvin 'Creepy' Karpis, one of Ma Baker's gang; although Karpis committed suicide in Spain, he is said to haunt the former prison bakery and kitchen.

Even Mark Twain was conscious of the island's odd atmosphere, describing it as being as cold as winter, even in the summer months.

The ghost of a man, apparently murdered while in solitary confinement, sometimes appears, stripped to the waist, in Cell 14D. After another prisoner was incarcerated in the same cell, he complained of being attacked by an entity with glowing green eyes. The prisoner was eventually found dead: he had been strangled, and there was fingermark bruising around his neck.

The following day, a body count of inmates was made, when it was discovered that there was one prisoner too many; could it have been that the ghost had also been counted?

Three prisoners who attempted escape, but eventually died in the prison, haunt the utility corridor in Block C, while another ghost has been reported in the Michigan Avenue cell block. The apparition stares fixedly at its beholder and noxious smells, crashing noises and screams accompany the event.

What remains of the warden's house is also believed to be haunted. It appears that a group of guards were playing cards there several years ago, when a phantom presence joined them in the game, and dealt out cards; the guards fled in terror.

One of the most bizarre sightings took place in the 1950s. The warden's wife was hanging out her washing to dry when she saw 50 or 60 soldiers by the shoreline, wearing the uniforms of the Civil War. An administrative worker also saw the soldiers, and they both heard cannons being fired. Neither of them knew that Alcatraz had been a Civil War fort.

Others claim to have seen the lighthouse, visible through the mist, that was demolished many years before.

ST. AUGUSTINE, FLORIDA

The Old Spanish military hospital in St. Augustine, Florida, was originally a church, known as Our Lady of Guadalupe, but the buildings that exist today are replicas of the originals. This has not prevented hauntings from continuing on the site, however, which is believed to have previously been a Timucuan burial ground.

St. Augustine, Florida, has many historic buildings, none more so than the Castillo de San Marcos, a fort originating from the 17th century. It symbolizes the culture clashes which ultimately resulted in America's unification, and is the site of many supernatural phenomena.

The Timucuans were a Native American people who once lived in Florida and parts of Georgia. Theirs was a thriving culture, which was devastated, after the arrival of the Spanish, by disease and war. Only a handful of Timacuans were left by the time the United States acquired Florida in 1821, and as an entity, the tribe has now ceased to exist. The Timacuans are described as being heavily tattooed, and the men, their hair worn in buns on top of their heads, were almost a head taller than the Spanish invaders.

The burial site is said to date from between 1100 and 1300, and has yielded much pottery and two full human skeletons. Psychic investigations have also taken place, during which four witnesses saw a garden stake being thrown across a room at one of the researchers. After a visit, some people found they had scratch marks on their backs, while others have seen objects been moved. Some are certain they have seen strange orbs, and even claim to have photographed the phenomena.

THE WINCHESTER MANSION, SAN JOSE, CALIFORNIA

Everyone knows that Winchester is the name of the famous repeating rifle, often described as the 'gun that won the West'. On 30 September 1862, at the height of the Civil War, William Wirt Winchester, the heir to the

128

Winchester Repeating Arms Company, married Sarah Pardee of New Haven. Their daughter, Annie, was born four years later, but died very soon afterwards. Sarah was obviously deeply affected, and for some time seemed to be on the brink of madness. As if to compound her anguish, a second tragedy occurred when William, now heir to the Winchester empire, died of tuberculosis on 7 March 1881, leaving Sarah an extremely rich widow.

Sarah was inconsolable, having lost the whole of her immediate family. A friend suggested she consult a Spiritualist medium, who told her that her family was cursed. Thousands of people had been killed by Winchester rifles and their spirits were crying out for vengeance.

Shortly after the séance, Sarah, believing she was being guided by her husband from beyond the grave, left New Haven and moved west to California. She reached the Santa Clara Valley in 1884, where she bought a six-roomed house under construction, ditched the original plans for it and substituted her own. For the next 36 years, she frenziedly continued to expand the house, using what the medium had termed 'blood money', and adding a maze of rooms and staircases that seemed to lead nowhere.

Sarah had become convinced that every person who had been killed by a Winchester rifle now haunted the house and that only by continuing to build would they be silenced. She hoped that by creating such a complex building the spirits would not find her.

She seems to have co-existed with the ghosts, somehow, and slept in a different room each night, which was no difficult matter because, by now, the house had 160 rooms. She became obsessed with the number 13 and used

OPPOSITE ABOVE: The famous Winchester repeat rifle that once belonged to Jesse James.

OPPOSITE BELOW: Sarah Winchester's woes were exacerbated by a medium, when he suggested that her family had been cursed by those killed by Winchester rifles.

LEFT: Theodore Roosevelt visited the Winchester Mansion in 1903, only to be turned away by Sarah, who by now was seriously deranged.

the motif in various combinations throughout the house, in the hope of warding off the malevolent spirits. Theodore Roosevelt paid a visit in 1903, but was told by Sarah that he could not enter because the house was only open to ghosts.

At the age of 83, Sarah died, and the house, having survived the San Francisco earthquake of 1906, is now a California Historical Landmark, described as 'a large, odd dwelling with an unknown number of rooms'. In the years that the house has been open to the public, employees, visitors and assorted psychics have had unusual encounters. Footsteps, banging doors,

organ music, mysterious voices, windows that are banged so hard that they shatter, cold spots, strange moving lights, doorknobs that turn by themselves – all of these phenomena seem to have been experienced at one time or another.

THE ALAMO (MISSION OF SAN ANTONIO DE VALERO, SAN ANTONIO, TEXAS)

San Antonio de Valero, established in 1718, was one of a chain of Catholic missions established by Spanish Franciscan monks to convert the Native Americans and colonize northern New Spain. It remained active as a mission until 1793, when it was dissolved, and its lands and buildings were distributed among the local people. A company of Spanish cavalry, sent to protect the settlements around San Antonio, later established its quarters in the old mission building.

On 23 February 1836, as part of the continuing Texan War of Independence, and in rebellion against Mexico's self-appointed dictator, General Santa Anna, Colonel William B. Travis arrived at the head of a force of 189 Texan volunteers to reinforce the defenders already inside the

garrison. By now it had been renamed the Alamo, and for the next 13 days was the site of a bloody siege, in which the legendary William Travis, Davy Crockett, Jim Bowie, and nearly all of the other defenders died to a man.

Despite the tragic Texan loss, the progress of the Mexican army had been slowed down, which allowed

OPPOSITE & BELOW: The Alamo, scene of one of the most tragic sieges in America's history.

Sam Houston to gather troops and supplies for his later successful battle at San Jacinto, in which the Texans won the war

Ghosts of disfigured men can be seen walking through the walls to this day, and some claim to have seen Travis and Bowie, while men on horseback are also seen, and screams can be heard coming from the Alamo at night.

THE BANK OF ENGLAND, LONDON

Sarah Whitehead's brother, Philip, was employed by the Bank of England but was accused of being a forger. He was arrested, convicted and hanged in 1811.

BELOW LEFT: The Bank of England is referred to as the 'Old Lady of Threadneedle Street'.

OPPOSITE: Liverpool St. Station, London – Bedlam's original site.

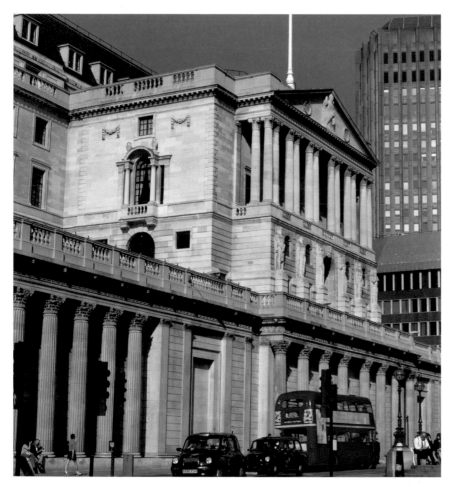

The events seemed to have unhinged Sarah's mind and every day for the next 25 years, until she died in 1836, she visited the bank to enquire after her brother. Her ghost haunts the small garden that is located in the centre of the building.

Yet another bizarre haunting is linked with this building. Many years ago, a truly enormous giant of a man worked in the bank as a cashier. He was gripped by the morbid fear that his body would eventually be taken by the Resurrectionists, and tried to convince the governors to let his body be buried within the bank, in order to protect it when he died. They appear to have acceded to his wishes, because later on, when workmen were making alterations to the building, they discovered a lead coffin, said to be 8ft long, with a stout iron chain fastened around it. Since then, the ghost of an exceptionally tall man has been seen in the area from time to time.

BEDLAM, LONDON

In 1247, Bethlem Royal Hospital was founded in London as a priory dedicated to St. Mary of Bethlehem. For most of its history, however, it was used as an asylum for the insane – also known as Bedlam   a word that came to be used for lunatic asylums in general, or to describe a scene of uproar and confusion. It was originally situated on the site of what is now Liverpool Street Station, but from 1675 to 1815 was sited at Moorfields, before being moved to ground on which the Imperial War Museum now stands. During the Second World War, a barrage balloon unit was stationed in the grounds of the museum, and its members reported hearing cries and groans and the rattling of chains.

One of the many stories that may explain the Bedlam-related hauntings dates to 1780, when a servant girl, called Rebecca, fell in love with her master. One day, he thanked her for her services, and slipping a golden guinea into her hand, told her he was going away. The casual rejection sent the girl insane and she was admitted to Bedlam, where she spent the rest of her life, holding the coin that would pay for her funeral. An attendant prised it from her still-warm fingers when she died, and Rebecca's wild-eyed ghost was later seen, seemingly searching for the stolen coin. Attendants and patients were, on occasions, confronted with Rebecca's ghost, which screamed at them to return her money. When the asylum was transferred to Lambeth Road in 1815, the ghost of Rebecca moved with it, where she presumably continued her long search.

BLICKLING HALL, NORFOLK, ENGLAND

Sir John Fastolfe (immortalized as Falstaff by William Shakespeare) sold Blickling Hall to his neighbour Geoffrey Boleyn in 1437. In 1505 it was inherited by Geoffrey's grandson, Sir Thomas Boleyn, whose daughter Anne became the second wife of King Henry VIII. She was executed in 1536 for alleged infidelities, though more likely it was for her inability to give Henry a son and heir.

The ghost of Anne Boleyn has been seen in many places (see also page 145, The Tower of London), but her appearances in the place where she was born are possibly the best documented. At Blickling Hall, her family home, she has been seen as a headless apparition on the anniversary of her execution:

BELOW: Blickling Hall in Norfolk, England, the family home of Anne Boleyn.

OPPOSITE: Buckingham Palace, once the seat of the dukes of Buckingham, now Queen Elizabeth II's London residence.

sometimes she is sitting, holding her own severed head in her lap, while at other times, around the midnight hour, she appears, headless, in a coach driven by a headless coachman and four headless horses.

When the National Trust for England, Wales and Northern Ireland took over the building in 1946, one of its administrators clearly saw Anne's ghost, wearing a long, grey gown with a white lace collar. He asked if he could help her, to which the apparition replied, 'that for which I seek has long since gone'.

Anne Boleyn was seen yet again in 1985, when the caretaker was awoken by the sound of footsteps in the passageway outside the bedroom he shared with his wife. He listened as the footsteps grew louder, then heard them cross a thin mat, lying across the doorway, and enter the room. Whoever it was, seemed to be standing at the foot of the bed, and the husband assumed it was his wife, returning from the bathroom. He flicked on the light and to his horror saw that his wife was sound asleep beside him – otherwise the room was empty. Only the following day did they learn that it had been the anniversary of Anne Boleyn's execution.

BUCKINGHAM PALACE, LONDON

Buckingham Palace evolved from a town house that was owned from the beginning of the 18th century by the dukes of Buckingham. It is said to be

suicide at the beginning of the 20th century after a divorce scandal. When the publicity became too much for the major, he blew his brains out in his first-floor office, from which phantom gunshots continue to be heard.

CHEYNE WALK, CHELSEA, LONDON

In Tudor times, the area where Cheyne Walk now stands, next to the River Thames, was part of a royal estate. The ghost of a bear, that haunted the garden of a house in Cheyne Walk as late as the mid-1920s, seems to have originated from the time when bear-

haunted by the ghost of a monk, who died in a punishment cell of the priory, that originally stood on the site until 1539. He appears at Christmastide, wearing his brown habit and dragging his iron chains, on the rear terrace of the palace. He moans as he walks up and down for a few minutes, and then he disappears.

The palace is also haunted by Major John Gwynne, a private secretary to King Edward VII, who committed

baiting was practised in England. It is believed that there was a bear pit in the vicinity until the 16th century, and a bear has also been sighted at the Tower of London.

The novelist, George Eliot, whose major works include *The Mill on the Floss* (1860), *Silas Marner* (1861), *Middlemarch* (1871–72), and *Daniel Deronda* (1876), died at number 4 Cheyne Walk in December 1880. A friend of hers, Katharine Macqoid, saw her standing at the bottom of her bed and was puzzled as to why this had occurred. She later discovered that George Eliot had died that same night.

The King's Head and Eight Bells is also situated on Cheyne Walk, and the unseen presence haunting the building,

OPPOSITE LEFT: Cheyne Walk, Chelsea, was part of the royal estate in Tudor times.

OPPOSITE RIGHT: The King's Head & Eight Bells, once a pub and now a brasserie, is reputedly haunted by unseen presences.

RIGHT: George Eliot died at no. 4 Cheyne Walk, her ghost appearing to her friend the night she died.

which no longer functions as a pub and is now a brasserie, was said to have caused the landlord and his wife many problems, in that the ghost became particularly active when a new member of staff was taken on, especially if that person was a female. Witnesses have felt someone brush past them, particularly on the stairs, and objects have been inexplicably moved around. The phantom's other activities include turning on gas cylinders in the cellar and switching off the central heating system.

CLEOPATRA'S NEEDLE, LONDON

Cleopatra's Needles are a pair of granite obelisks, brought from Egypt in 1878. One was set up on the Thames Embankment in London, and the other now stands in Central Park, New York. Neither are connected with the legendary Cleopatra VII, though both bear her name. In fact, the London obelisk was constructed for Tuthmose III (reigned 1504–1450 BC) and is carved with hieroglyphics praising the pharaoh, while later inscriptions were added by Ramesses the Great to commemorate his victories.

Somewhat nonsensically, the London obelisk is reputed to have been

OPPOSITE: Cleopatra's Needle, London, its twin being in Central Park, New York.

RIGHT: In recent times, Thomas Wolsey's ghost has manifested itself at Hampton Court Palace.

BELOW RIGHT: Hampton Court Palace.

cursed by Cleopatra. However, a strange, silent apparition, thought to be the ghost of one of the many people who have committed suicide on the spot, has been seen on numerous occasions. The apparition is described as being male, tall and naked, and witnesses have seen him jump from the parapet, near to the obelisk, hitting the water silently and making no splash. Others have reported hearing strange laughter and moaning in the vicinity.

HAMPTON COURT PALACE, ENGLAND

Numerous ghosts haunt the palace, all of them famous individuals, who in one way or another had strong connections with the place. Hampton Court is situated approximately 12 miles (19km) upstream from London on the River Thames. Cardinal Thomas Wolsey,

Henry VIII's chief advisor, began to rebuild the original 14th-century manor house in 1514, laying down the basis of the building as it is today. When he fell out of favour, however, Wolsey was forced to relinquish the palace to his monarch. It is claimed that an apparition, thought to be Cardinal Wolsey, was seen during a public performance held at the palace in 1966.

Catherine Howard also haunts the building. After Henry VIII discovered his queen's infidelity, she spent many hours in the chapel praying for forgiveness. Allegedly, she was physically held down on the execution

block on 13 February 1542; since then, witnesses have heard her fists banging on the chapel door, heard her screams pleading for her life, and seen her walking in the gardens. She has often been seen in the Long Gallery, where she appears to be fleeing from an unknown pursuer, which led to the gallery being closed some time in the 19th century.

Jane Seymour appears as a lady in white, walking through the Clock Court and the Silver Stick Gallery, candle in hand. She died of an infection following childbirth in 1537, having provided Henry with a son and heir, the future

Edward VI. She is usually seen on 12 October, the anniversary of Prince Edward's birth.

The ghost of Sybil Penn, who died in 1562 of smallpox and was buried in the old church, has also been seen. She was Edward VI's nurse until he died, aged 16, in 1553. She did not begin to haunt the building until her tomb was moved in 1821. Suddenly her voice could be heard in the hallways, and once again the whirring of her spinning wheel was heard, coming from a wall in the south-west wing. Sybil Penn has also been

LEFT & BELOW: The ghosts of Catherine Howard and Jane Seymore, two of Henry VIII's wives, are also reputed to haunt Hampton Court.

OPPOSITE: The inner courtyard of Hampton Court Palace.

PAGE 142–143: Caernarfon Castle is possibly the most striking medieval monument in Wales. It is said to be haunted by the ghosts of English soldiers, also of a floating woman, sighted in 2001.

sighted at Penn Place, that was once her former home.

Towards the end of the last century, two skeletons were discovered, buried in a shallow grave beneath a doorway, following a number of night-time disturbances.

During the First World War, a police officer on duty at the palace saw two men and eight women standing by the front gate. He could hear the sound of the women's rustling dresses before all melted into thin air.

NEWGATE PRISON, LONDON
The prison was situated at the corner of Newgate Street and Old Bailey, just inside the City of London. It got its

The Old Bailey Central Criminal Court, London. Between Newgate Prison and the Old Bailey was a small, completely enclosed passageway, called Birdcage Walk, which led to the lime pits, where the remains of prisoners were buried. The Old Bailey itself is said to be haunted by a shadowy spectre, which often appears after a serious trial has taken place.

name from the fifth gate that was added to the other entrances in the wall that surrounded the city, hence the 'new gate'. The original prison was built in 1188 and rebuilt in 1770. It was badly damaged during the Gordon Riots in 1780, following which a new prison was commissioned that was completed in 1782.

In 1783, the site of London's gallows was moved from Tyburn to Newgate, where public executions continued to draw large crowds. A new scaffold was built outside so that 12 men could be executed at the same time. The prison was demolished in 1902 to make way for the Central Criminal Court.

Between Newgate and the Old Bailey was a small, completely enclosed passageway, called Birdcage Walk (or Dead Man's Walk), which led to the lime pits, where the remains of

executed prisoners were buried. Jack Shepherd, the notorious cat burglar, was hanged here in November 1724, having escaped custody three times. Witnesses have seen a dark shape in Dead Man's Walk late at night, believed to be Shepherd's ghost, and have also heard the sounds of chains rattling and heavy footsteps.

The ivy-covered wall at the end of Amen Court, that backed on to the old Newgate Prison and its graveyard, and which is thought to have been the route by which prisoners sometimes escaped, is thought to be haunted by a particularly unpleasant manifestation, known for centuries as the Black Dog of Newgate. This was witnessed crawling along the top of the wall immediately before an execution was about to take place. A prisoner, Luke Hutton, wrote that he believed it to be the ghost of a former prisoner, called Scholler, who had been eaten by the other starving prisoners.

The ghost of Amelia Dyer, the 19th-century baby-farmer, has also been seen on the site. She is reported to have said to Scott, the Chief Warder, on her way to the scaffold on 10 June 1896, 'I'll meet you again, some day, sir.' Some time later, Scott was sitting in

the keeper's room when he saw the face of Amelia framed in the grille of the door. He leapt up and opened the door, but there was nothing to be seen, apart from a woman's handkerchief left lying on the floor; there had been no women prisoners at Newgate for years. Scott was photographed outside the prison soon after, and it is said that the face of Amelia appeared on the print, once the film had been developed.

THE TOWER OF LONDON

Although the Tower of London reflects Britain's royal heritage, it has long been associated with cruelty and bloodshed; the events that occurred in places such as the Bloody Tower, Traitors Gate and the dungeon called 'Little Ease', have made it the most haunted place in England.

Those who were incarcerated in the Tower of London played an important part in Britain's history, but conspiracy and the struggle for power led to their demise, and many were interrogated, tortured, and sentenced without a trial. Countless victims were executed on Tower Hill, outside the Tower of London, and only seven were executed within its walls on Tower Green, three of whom were queens of England.

Dominating the flat countryside of East Anglia, the magnificent Ely Cathedral, 'the ship of the Fens', began life as a Saxon monastery for nuns and monks until the Viking invasion of 869 left it completely destroyed. Some 100 years later, the site was reconsecrated as a Benedictine monastery, but it was not until late in the 11th century that work began on the present structure, which dates from 1082. A cathedral since 1109, Ely has seen many deaths, including those of the people who built it.

There have been many ghostly sightings. During the restoration of the cathedral in the 1990s, workers reported seeing monk-like figures walking in the grounds and on the staircase of the bell tower. There have also been strange phenomena, such as tools going missing only to reappear later on.

Undoubtably the most haunted area is what is now the cathedral's gift shop, where sudden chills and cold spots can be felt.

These were Anne Boleyn and Catherine Howard, two of the wives of Henry VIII, and Lady Jane Grey, who was queen for only a few days. All were killed by beheading, and five of the seven are reputed to haunt the Tower.

Sir Thomas à Becket (1118–70), an archbishop of Canterbury, was assassinated by four knights in his cathedral, when they took the words, uttered in anger by King Henry II, as a firm command. Becket's ghost is said to have struck the Traitor's Gate twice, reducing it to rubble, while poltergeist activity has been reported in the room dedicated to his memory: this takes the form of doors opening and closing of their own accord, the sound of a monk's sandals flapping against the floor, and that of an unknown child crying.

Henry VI was imprisoned in the Wakefield Tower and was killed by an unknown hand on 21 May 1471. His ghostly apparition can be seen on the anniversary of his death, when he is said to pace around the room. He looks pitiful, with his sad, wan face, and when the clock completes its midnight chimes he disappears into the walls.

In the Bloody Tower, the ghosts of Edward V and his brother, Richard,

Duke of York, more often referred to as the Princes in the Tower, and possibly murdered by their uncle, Richard III in around 1483, have been seen standing hand-in-hand, clad only in their nightgowns. Their skeletons were discovered in 1674, when they were given a proper burial at last.

Both Cardinal Wolsey and Thomas Wentworth, Earl of Strafford, have also appeared in years gone by to those awaiting execution within the confines of the Tower.

OPPOSITE: The Tower of London not only reflects the richness of the British heritage, but also the cruelty of its power struggles.

ABOVE: Lady Jane Grey was queen for only a few days before losing her head.

Anne Boleyn haunts the Queen's House, where she was confined until her execution in 1536, having been seen by several different people, including sentries, who attempted to

The shadow of an executioner's axe is said to pass over Tower Green and come to rest on the White Tower. This is allegedly connected with the execution of Cardinal Pole's mother, Margaret, the Countess of Salisbury, in 1541. The screams that have been heard in the area are thought to be the re-enactment of her execution, when she fought with the executioner, who chased her around the scaffold. Guards within the White Tower have also experienced ghostly happenings: one man felt as though he was being crushed, while another had a black cloak flung over his head and

attack the apparition with bayonets. She appears here on 19 May, the anniversary of her death, and is also seen outside the chapel; beefeaters have also reported strange lights flickering in the middle of the night, while others have seen a procession of Tudor courtiers gliding down the aisle of the chapel, led by a headless woman, who disappears into a wall.

George Boleyn, Viscount Rochford, was the brother of Anne Boleyn. He was charged with committing incest with her and was executed, as also was his sister, in 1536. He was hung, drawn and quartered in the Tower, since when his phantom is said to haunt the upper rooms.

twisted around his neck; a third man was spoken to by an unseen presence.

Northumberland's Walk is haunted by the ghost of John Dudley, Duke of Northumberland, who walked here prior to his execution. Edward VI, the young son of Henry VIII, had complete trust in the duke, and at Dudley's insistence, passed over his half-sisters, Mary and Elizabeth, making Lady Jane Grey, Dudley's daughter-in-law, his heir. When Edward died, possibly poisoned by Dudley, the duke boldly proclaimed Jane queen.

Guildford Dudley's ghost has been seen both in the Beauchamp Tower and on Tower Hill. He was the 5th son of

John Dudley and was married to Lady Jane Grey. He was tried at Guildhall on 13 November 1553 and found guilty of treason. It is reported that he wept on his way to the scaffold. Lady Jane Grey has also been seen in the Beauchamp Tower. She watched her husband being executed and her apparition re-enacts her own fate, completed on the same day. She has been sighted on the anniversary of her execution, when she is seen floating on a cloud of shimmering mist and gliding along the battlements before eventually disappearing from view.

The Salt Tower was the final resting place of Henry Walpole, who was imprisoned in the Tower in 1593 for the crime of being a Catholic priest. He was frequently and severely racked,

OPPOSITE ABOVE LEFT: Henry VI haunts the Wakefield Tower, his ghost appearing on the anniversary of his death.

OPPOSITE ABOVE RIGHT & CENTRE: Elizabeth I and Henry VIII.

ABOVE: The Traitor's Gate, through which prisoners brought by boat were transported to the Tower of London.

before being hung, drawn and quartered on 7 April 1595. It is not known for sure if the strange yellow glow that fills the room is connected with him, but visitors have heard prayers being recited in a low whisper, and felt the ice-cold touch of fingers on their necks.

Sir Walter Raleigh's ghost appears as a seemingly solid form, seen momentarily before it disappears from view. He was imprisoned in the Tower

from 1603 until 1618, and yeomen have seen him peering into their guardroom.

In 1605 a band of Catholic extremists devised the Gunpowder Plot, a scheme to kill James I and as many members of James's parliament as possible. The plan was to make Henry VIII's young daughter, Elizabeth, queen, and in time arrange Elizabeth's marriage to a Catholic nobleman. The plot was discovered and Thomas Percy, who was a party to the conspiracy, was executed along with the others. The unseen hands of Thomas Percy, who was imprisoned in the Martin Tower, are said to push unsuspecting visitors down the steps.

A face has been seen peering out of one of the windows of St. Thomas's Tower by staff and visitors, while in a single sighting in the Martin Tower in 1817, Edmund Swifte saw a glass tube, which turned from white to blue.

Ghostly choirs have also been heard and numerous other manifestations have been reported, including white smoke emanating from one of the cannons, which appeared to change its shape.

The sound of pacing footsteps has often been heard in the Middle Tower,

going back and forth along the battlements.

The Tower also boasts the ghost of a bear: in 1864 a soldier saw the apparition and lunged at it with his bayonet. It is believed that the ghost is a throwback to the days when bear-baiting took place in the grounds of the Tower.

The Byward Tower was the scene of a sighting in the 1980s, when a yeoman, on duty during the night, saw two beefeaters dressed in clothes from a much earlier period. They were talking animatedly to one another, while smoking their pipes, one sitting on either side of the fireplace.

A 'strange-looking figure' has been seen very close to the area where executions used to take place. The man, wearing drab clothes that the witness assumed were of the Second World War utility type, was seen walking with a bowed head, but vanished shortly afterwards.

The Byward Tower, one of five towers flanking the Tower of London, gives access to the Outer Ward. It is here that the password is still demanded by the sentry at night.

Arundel Castle, located close to the South Downs in some of England's most beautiful countryside, was established at the time of the Norman conquest, but on what may have been earlier foundations. It has been home to the dukes of Norfolk since the 1500s.

Three ghosts are said to haunt the castle, the first being that of a man seen in the library. The second is of a young girl, who committed suicide by jumping from the Hiorne Tower, while the third haunts the servants' quarters. The latter was seen in 1958 by a trainee footman, who saw only the head and shoulders of a youngish man wearing a loose-sleeved tunic.

Palace House, which overlooks the Beaulieu village from across the Beaulieu river in Hampshire, England, was began in 1204 as the gatehouse to Beaulieu Abbey. It has been the ancestral home of a branch of the Montagu family since 1538, when it was bought from the crown following the Dissolution of the Monasteries by Henry VIII. Having been extended throughout the centuries, it is now a fine example of a Gothic country house.

Beaulieu is one of Britain's most haunted places, and over the last 100 years there have been many reports of sightings and unseen presences. The Reverend Robert Frazer Powles was the Vicar of Beaulieu between 1886 and 1939, and reported seeing so many ghostly monks that he began to take them for granted, making such comments as 'Brother Simon was here again last night. I heard his boots squeak'. In Palace House, particularly in the upstairs rooms, many have reported smelling incense, which is thought to portend that a member of the Montagu family is in imminent danger.

The Grey Lady is said to be Isabella, Countess of Beaulieu, who died in 1786. She is a noisy ghost and walks through walls in the private apartments. She has also been seen by visitors, who mistake her for a costumed guide.

CHAPTER FOUR

GHOSTLY CREATURES

SPECTRAL HOUNDS

The animal most commonly seen in ghostly form is a black dog, sometimes referred to as a hell-hound, a dog of doom, or a Church Grim. Such a creature is central to the famous Sherlock Holmes novel, *The Hound of the Baskervilles*, that was possibly based on the Black Shuck of East Anglia, even though the action of the story takes place in England's West Country.

Tales of these spectral hounds date back hundreds of years and are told the length and breadth of Britain. One of the most recent, perhaps, is the one connected with the death of the British composer, Lionel Monckton, who died in 1924.

One day, some of Monckton's friends, including Donald Calthrop, were sitting chatting in their club, when Calthrop had a sudden premonition that all was not right as

The Church Grim, one of many types of spectral hound, was said to protect graveyards from the Devil,

tragic news arrived that Monckton had died – apparently at the precise moment of Calthrop's sighting of the black dog.

But there was an even more terrifying manifestation on 4 August 1577, in Bungay, Suffolk. Most of the townsfolk were gathered together in St. Mary's Church, when a violent thunderstorm was suddenly unleashed. Suddenly, a black dog appeared, illuminated by the intermittant bursts of lightning. Everyone saw the creature as it ran down the aisle, and two people died of fright where they knelt in prayer. A third was also affected, and although they survived, they were left shrivelled and bent. The church tower collapsed in through the roof and the church's north door was left with scorchmarks, that can be seen to this day.

FAR LEFT: Dartmoor, Devon. This was the setting for Conan Doyle's Hound of the Baskervilles, *based on East Anglia's legendary Black Shuck.*

ABOVE LEFT: The appearance of the Black Dog of Bungay, Suffolk, made such an impression on the locals, that is appears on items throughout the town.

far as Monckton was concerned. He was suddenly aware of a black dog, standing in the corner of the room. His companions did not share the experience, however, and dismissed it as imagination. A few hours later, the

What they had seen was the fearful creature known as the Black Shuck. Described as a devil-dog, it has been seen wandering the East Anglian

ABOVE: The remains of Bungay Castle, once the home of Hugh Bigod.

RIGHT: The magnificent church of the Holy Trinity at Blythburgh, Suffolk. It is also known as the Cathedral of the Marshes, and was founded in 1125.

countryside since Viking times, being a large dog, sometimes as big as a horse, with malevolent flaming eyes that glow red or green.

The Black Shuck also seems to have connections with Hugh Bigod, the Earl of Norfolk, who staged a rebellion against Henry II in 1173. Legend has it that to guarantee his success he made a pact with the Devil, forfeiting his soul. The Devil tricked him, however, and his army was defeated, forcing him to

surrender his property, that included Bungay Castle. He challenged the Devil, however, who by way of compromise, transformed him into a black devil-dog.

Blythburgh Church in Suffolk, a magnificent building known as the Cathedral of the Marshes, also bears the scorchmarks of Black Shuck on its door, when, as at Bungay, he attempted to enter. This time, it seems, the power of prayer was able to save the parishioners.

A black dog is also associated with Peel Castle, on the Isle of Man, where sightings of the apparition became so frequent that the guards came to accept it as a normal occurrence. The creature is supposed to haunt the underground passages and may be echoing early pagan rituals once held in the vicinity.

LEFT: The Angel of the East. The village of Blythburgh is littered with references to angels, so it came as no surprise when the locals decided to commemorate the millennium by having a large angel built in metal.

OPPOSITE: Black Shuck's scorchmarks are still visible on the door of Blythburgh's church.

In 1907, at Budleigh Hill in Somerset, another black dog, with 'great big fiery eyes as big as saucers', was seen, while in Yorkshire, the black dog, known there as the Barguest, has been seen in a limestone gorge known as Troller's Gill, near to the village of Applewick in the heart of the Dales.

The road from St. Audreis to Perry Farm, in Somerset, is haunted by a black dog, that appears to presage an imminent death in the vicinity. In Hatfield Peverel, in Essex, a wagon is reported to have struck a ghostly black dog on a country lane, causing it to explode and set fire to the driver and his wagon.

In the North of England, the black dog is referred to as Padfoot, and in Burnley in Lancashire as Shriker or Trach. They are said to appear to people who are about to die and are described as large, shaggy creatures with broad feet. A headless black dog is said to have appeared outside an old church in Manchester in 1825. It rested its paws on the shoulders of a tradesman, called Drabble, which, understandably, caused him to flee.

The noted English poet, novelist and biographer, Penelope Fitzgerald, once worked in a bookshop in

Southwold, Suffolk. She was to prove the exception to the rule that not all ghostly dogs are black, having seen a spectral hound that was large and white. She was walking a pony across Walberswick Common, when the creature, approaching soundlessly through the dry bracken, suddenly confronted her. It disappeared as abruptly as it had appeared, but she later learned that a white dog had been seen waiting for its owner there for over a century.

Ghostly hounds are not only confined to England. In fact, one of the best documented cases occurred in the U.S. The American writer of dog stories, Albert Terhune, once owned a collie called Rex. The dog died in 1916 and some time afterwards the Reverend Appleton Grannis came to stay at Terhune's home at Sunnybank, in Wayne, New Jersey. The clergyman had not visited for some time and was not aware of Rex's existence. One day, Grannis saw a dog looking in through the window. He described it in great detail, and Terhune immediately realized it was Rex, down to the last scar on the dog's face. The dog appeared several more times, and the family noted that the other dogs in

the household deliberately avoided what, in life, had been Rex's favourite sleeping place.

In Sarina, Western Australia, in 1953, William Courtney was obliged to have his dog, Lady, destroyed. That very night, he thought he heard Lady

LEFT: There have been so many sightings of a black dog at Peel Castle, on the Isle of Man, that guards now take the phenomenon for granted.

ABOVE: A black dog, rather like this, perhaps, is known as Padfoot in the North of England.

GHOSTLY CREATURES

THE MONKEY OF DRUMLANRIG CASTLE

One of the most bizarre stories featuring an animal is that of the so-called Monkey of Drumlanrig Castle. Only the cellars remain of the original 14th-century castle, where Mary, Queen of Scots stayed in 1563 and

in the hallway. The sounds continued, and then he heard the familiar sound as the dog lay down on the floor next to his bed.

Twenty-one years later, on the other side of the world, in Helsinki, Finland, Pia Virtakallio clearly saw the ghost of her boxer dog, Cherry, standing looking at her. This was thoroughly peculiar, not only because the dog had died two years earlier, at the age of 11, but also because it appeared very much younger, being now not much more than a pup.

Bonnie Prince Charlie in 1745, after his unsuccessful invasion of England. The mansion now standing on the site was built in the 1700s for William Douglas, the first Duke of Queensberry, and its ownership later passed to the dukes of Buccleuch.

The mansion is haunted by three ghosts: that of a yellow monkey, that has been seen several times, though it was only recognized as a monkey recently; that of Lady Anne Douglas, seen carrying her severed head; and that of a little girl, who has been seen in a bedroom, floating a few feet above the floor.

There is also reputed to be the blood of a murder victim on the floor of one of the passageways, which, however one may try, cannot be washed away – a motif that commonly occurs in folklore.

RIGHT: The Scottish Highlands, where black frogs were said to be household familiars.

OPPOSITE LEFT: A witch, transformed into a hare, haunts Bolingbroke Castle.

OPPOSTE RIGHT: A large black cat haunts the Dower House at Killackee.

possibly a throwback to a time when such animals were brought back home from far-off lands as trophies.

OTHER PHANTOM CREATURES

Strange black frogs have been seen in the Scottish Highlands, while the bizarre spirit of a witch appears in the form of a hare at Bolingbroke Castle in Lincolnshire. In Killackee, in the Republic of Ireland, a large, black cat the size of a dog haunts the Dower House, later used by Margaret O'Brien as an arts centre. A vast black bird has been seen since the middle of the 18th century at Drayton Church, near Uxbridge, a suburb of London. The bird sits on a coffin in one of the vaults, pecking away at the wood.

Even more bizarrely, at the Theatre Royal in Bath, there is a phantom butterfly. It was first seen in 1948, when a Christmas production included a butterfly ballet, since when it has appeared in successive productions.

Documents, dating to the 1700s, hinted at a haunted room at Drumlanrig, referred to as the 'yellow-monkey room'. The building was used as a hospital during the First World War, where the matron is reputed to have seen a terrifying apparition of a monkey or ape, causing her immediately to leave her post.

Lady Alice Montague-Douglas-Scott, who later became Princess Alice, Duchess of Gloucester (1901–2004), claimed to her dying day to have seen a massive ape, sitting on one of the chairs in a passageway. The manifestation was

BELOW: A vast black bird has been seen since the middle of the 18th century at Drayton Church, near Uxbridge, London.

RIGHT: The Tower of London.

Among the Tower of London's dozens of apparitions, is a phantom bear. In around 1815 a sentry, given the task of guarding the Crown Jewels, saw the dark form of a large bear coming towards him up a flight of steps. He thrust at the animal, but his bayonet passed straight through, jamming itself into the wood of a door. The sentry collapsed and the next day died, having been 'the victim of a shadow'.

LEFT: The headless ghost of a dog, not seen at the time, but which appeared on a photograph taken c.1916 by Arthur Springer, a retired CID inspector from Scotland Yard.

ABOVE: Close-up of a photograph of a family group, taken in August 1925 in Clarens, Switzerland, by Major Wilmot Allistone. When the film was developed, the head of a white kitten could be seen in the boy's hand, nestling against the toy rabbit he was already holding. It was recognized as a kitten belonging to the family, which had died some weeks earlier after it had been mauled by a dog.

CHAPTER FIVE
GHOSTLY TALES & LEGENDS

Tales of strange manifestations or phenomena, experienced by a succession of people over successive generations, seem to have stood the test of time. Many have read Charles Dickens's story, *A Christmas Carol*, published in 1843, which caused other writers to follow in his footsteps. Christmas ghost stories became a regular feature on both sides of the Atlantic, some of them echoing ghost stories that many perceived as true.

THE ANGELS OF MONS

The first major engagement between British and German forces during the First World War was at Mons in France, in August 1914, an action that Britain would find difficult to win. In April 1915, in the Spiritualist press, an account was published telling how supernatural forces had intervened on the side of Britain at a crucial moment in the battle.

This led to a plethora of similar rumours, including one, which as it turns out, was a work of fiction. Arthur Machen, a leader-writer on the *Evening News*, later maintained that these rumours had come from a story he had published in that paper on 29 September 1914, entitled 'The Bowmen'. It told how phantom bowmen, summoned from the Battle of Agincourt by St. George, fired their arrows at England's enemies. A significant number of people seem to have taken these stories as true, in what may possibly be a case of mass wish-fulfilment, occurring as a boost to morale in what was a grim period in British history.

THE GREEN LADY

In Banffshire, in Scotland, there is a valley associated with a Green Lady. According to legend, the ghost was first seen about six months after the death of the local laird's wife. One day, a ploughman came face to face with a woman, clad from head to toe in green, her face concealed by a large hood. There was something about the woman that terrified him, and his terror increased when she asked for a ride on his horse to cross a stream. But he agreed and she sprang up behind him with great agility. He described her as feeling like a half-filled sack of wool.

When the couple reached the other side, the woman dismounted, pulling aside her hood to reveal herself as the laird's dead wife. She promised she would see the man again before long.

Over the years, the Green Lady appeared to many of the servants, but never to the laird himself. Soon they became accustomed to her visits; they could hear her laughing and sometimes she threw pillows at the chambermaids. But she did not seem to be happy, and her face was very pale.

On one occasion she appeared to the family nurse, warning her that two of the laird's children were in grave danger on the seashore. The nurse told the laird and he rode to the coast just in time to save the children, who were hanging onto a rock. The nurse returned to her room and saw the Green Lady sitting beside her fire. They began to talk and the lady told her why she had returned.

Two years before her death, a peddler had apparently climbed into the orchard. The lady sent one of the servants to tell him to leave, but there was a scuffle in which the peddler died. They discovered that the man's pack held velvet, silk and a large number of gold coins, which she and the servant divided between themselves, burying the body in an unmarked grave. The lady hid her share of the gold behind a tapestry in her room, using the green silk to make the dress she now wore.

When the wall behind the tapestry was later examined, a cache of golden coins were found and in the place where the peddler had been buried, human remains were discovered.

THE STORY OF PETER RUGG

The idea of being compelled to wander for eternity, told in the legends of 'The Wandering Jew', 'The Flying Dutchman', and in the character of Kundry, in 'Parsifal', has parallels with the story of Peter Rugg.

Ghosts are not only confined to buildings, but also appear in the open air, as in the story of the Green Lady.

In 1826 William Austin tried to board a coach leaving Boston, Massachusetts, but it was so full that he was obliged to sit up beside the driver. They had barely left Boston when the horses became nervous, which, as the driver intimated, was because a storm was imminent.

The driver used the words 'storm-breeder', explaining that they described the ghost of a man in an open carriage,

Caerphilly Castle in Wales has its own Green Lady – the beautiful Princess Alice of Angoulême, the wife of Gilbert de Clare, who came with the Normans in 1066 and built the castle.

Starved of love by her husband, Alice fell in love with Gruffyd the Fair, Prince of Brithdir. The affair had to be kept secret, but Gruffyd confided in a monk who turned out to be in the employ of Gilbert, making him aware of his wife's treachery. Gilbert sent Alice back to France, and Gruffyd, on hearing the news, hanged the monk from a tree in what is known today as Ystrad Mynach (Monk's Vale).

Gilbert's men eventually caught up with Gryffyd and he too was hanged. Alice, in despair, died of a broken heart. Her ghost, dressed in green, is reputed to haunt the castle ramparts.

accompanied by a small girl. He had seen them on several occasions, after which thunder clouds would invariably begin to gather.

He told Austin that on one occasion the carriage stopped and the ghost asked him the way to Boston, to which the ghost had responded by pointing the wrong way. Since then, he had learned that the ghost had sought directions from other drivers, but always ignored their reply.

Sure enough, the carriage did stop, just as the driver had predicted, and Austin would meet the storm-breeder once again, three years later, when he was staying in a hotel in Hartford, Connecticut. One evening he was standing by the front porch and heard a man say: 'Here comes Peter Rugg and his child. He looks wet and weary and farther from Boston than ever.'

Moments later, the same carriage and driver appeared, with storm clouds following along behind, and this time it was headed straight for the hotel. The man Austin had overheard told him he had seen Rugg 20 years before, when he asked the way to Boston. He had told him he was driving in the wrong direction, but Rugg had said: 'Alas! It is all turn back! Boston

shifts with the wind and plays all around the compass. One man tells me it is to the east, another to the west, and the guideposts too, all point the wrong way!'

Austin could not stop himself from asking the driver if he was indeed Peter Rugg, to which the man replied that he was and that he lived on Middle Street in Boston. Austin could see that both Rugg and the child were soaking wet, even though it was not raining. Austin told Rugg that he was in Connecticut and that Boston was 100 miles away. Rugg seemed not to believe him, claimed he was within 40 miles of the city, and with that drove off.

Austin's meeting perplexed him greatly, leading him to investigate further. He found an old lady, Mrs. Croft, who lived on Middle Street. It seems that Peter Rugg had visited her and asked her whether a Mrs. Rugg lived in the house. The old woman replied that once she did, but that she had died many years before. Mrs. Croft advised Austin to go and see James Felt, who by that time was in his late 80s, but who knew of Peter Rugg from what he had been told by his grandfather.

Apparently, a Peter Rugg had lived on Middle Street in the 1730s. Felt's

grandfather had described Rugg as an ill-tempered man who would never take advice. One day he had gone out for a ride to Concord with his daughter. He stopped by a friend's house, and the friend warned him that a storm was brewing, to which Rugg had replied 'Let the storm increase. I will see home tonight in spite of the storm, or may I never see home!' This was the last time Rugg and his daughter were ever seen; they disappeared without a trace, seemingly doomed to travel for eternity.

LA LLORNA

The legend of La Llorna is said to date from the time of the conquistadors in America, being the spirit of a tall, thin, weeping woman. She had long, flowing black hair and wore a white gown. She is said to be looking for children to drag away into the night, so that they may join her in her watery grave.

La Llorna was once a peasant girl, called Maria, who married a wealthy man and produced two sons. Her husband was supposedly a womanizer and an alcoholic and had long since ceased to care for her. He threatened to leave her one day and marry someone belonging to his own class.

Maria was left largely to her own devices: one evening as she was out strolling with her children beside the river, they saw their father in a carriage with an elegant lady. Maria's husband stopped, spoke to the children, but ignored his wife before driving off. Maria was so enraged that she grabbed the children, ran down to the river, and threw them in. She was immediately remorseful and did all that she could to save them, but to no avail.

Maria refused to eat, growing thinner and thinner until she finally died. Her ghost can still be seen, doomed to be left crying eternally beside the Santa Fe river at dusk. She has also been seen floating among the trees along the river bank, crying out for her children, while others have seen her further afield, on the banks of the Yellowstone river in Montana.

The tale sometimes becomes that of a phantom hitchhiker. On several stretches of road, close to the Santa Fe

PAGES 180 & 181: The city of Boston has its fair share of ghost stories.

OPPOSITE: The Yellowstone river in Montana, where La Llorna is said to have appeared.

river, solitary drivers have reported seeing a weeping woman, standing beside the road. The driver pulls up, offers her a lift, to whom she tells her brief story before vanishing.

The fact that La Llorna is seen in so many different locations might partly explain the phenomena of phantom hitchhikers across the United States. On different occasions a young girl, wearing a white party dress, is seen. It is usually a rainy night on a deserted road, and the girl appears real enough, being wet through and shivering.

The driver takes her to the address she gives, but during the journey the girl disappears. Puzzled, the driver knocks on the door of the house, only to be told by the occupants that, yes indeed they had a daughter, but she had died in a car accident ten years before. Drivers have even been known to locate the daughter's grave, and having given the girl his jacket to keep her warm, it is sometimes found, neatly folded, beside that same grave.

There are three similar versions of this story. One, in fact, appeared in a December 1890 edition of a Russian newspaper, in which a priest, claiming to have been sent by a woman to an address to administer the last rites to a dying man, finds a young man instead. The priest recognizes a photograph or painting of the woman who directed him to the house, and when he asks who she is, the young man replies that it was his mother, but that she has been dead for several years. The man prays with the priest, thus sealing his own fate, and dies that very evening.

Similar incidents have occurred on numerous occasions in the United States, but they usually involve a doctor rather than a priest. The victim is always an otherwise healthy person, but as soon as the dead mother has sent the doctor to the address, they rapidly fall prey to disease.

It seems that this kind of legend appears all over the world. In Armenia, the tale is told of a rider who passes a cemetery and sees a young woman crying. She tells him she is too tired to travel, but needs to be far away by the morning. As luck would have it, the rider is always going to that particular destination. He gives her a ride on his horse and the girl does not speak. After a while, she appears to be growing heavier, as if she were falling asleep. Suddenly the horse stops and the girl falls off. The rider discovers she is dead and that for some time he has been carrying a corpse. The Armenians believe the tale signifies a girl who has died some distance from her home, and that on the anniversary of her death each year, she tries to return to her native village.

There is a German version of the La Llorna story, which involves the famous Lorelei Rock, situated on the River Rhine. At dusk, the rock transforms into a beautiful maiden, who sings a haunting song, luring anyone sailing on the river to certain death on the treacherous rock. Many ships and their crew have been lost here over the years.

Perhaps the story holds a grain of truth. Legend tells that Lorelei lived many years ago, and that she was in love with a knight, who left her to go to war. Many others courted her, but she could think only of this one man. Many men whom Lorelei spurned killed themselves, but her knight never returned. The Archbishop of Cologne decided to send her to a convent. On the way, she asked if she could stand on the rock, so that she could gaze for one last time at the knight's castle. Just as

OPPOSITE: The famous Lorelei Rock on the River Rhine in Germany.

she was doing this, a small boat came into view with the love of her life on board. She shouted his name and, transfixed by her beauty, the knight let the boat hit the rock and he subsequently drowned. Full of grief, Lorelei threw herself into the waters of the Rhine to join him.

As bizarre as the phantom hitchhikers are the stories of the radiant boys, believed to be the ghosts of children who were murdered by their parents. Tales of such children are told throughout Europe, but one of the best documented involves Viscount Castlereagh, an English statesman.

While hunting in Ireland as a young man, Castlereagh managed to find cover in a house just as a violent storm began to break. The house was full of fugitives from the storm, but the host assured Castlereagh that there was enough room for him. In the end, Castlereagh was given a mattress on the floor beside a huge fire. He fell asleep, and after a few hours was awoken by a bright light. By now the fire had died out, but the light was in fact coming from a beautiful young man. Castlereagh was terrified and in the morning told his host that he was leaving, explaining the reason why. The host swore he knew nothing of the apparition, and neither did the servants, until the butler was called.

The butler told Castlereagh that he had been sleeping in the boy's room and that he had taken the precaution of lighting a fire to keep him out. It then transpired that many years before, a boy of around nine or ten had been murdered by his mother, and that it had happened in that very room.

The host was terrified to hear this, especially when he heard that every time the apparition appeared to a person they were destined for a period of great success followed by a violent death.

Castlereagh was the second son of the Marquis of Londonderry, but soon afterwards his elder brother died, leaving Castlereagh as heir. In a short period of time Castlereagh became one of the most powerful men in Europe, even though he was a hated and deeply troubled man.

On 12 August 1822, having been confined to his country home because of his erratic behaviour, Castlereagh cut his own throat with a penknife.

KING ARTHUR

In the dark ages after the Romans left Britain, legend has it that one man, known as the once and future king,

BELOW & OPPOSITE: Glastonbury, one of the supposed resting places of King Arthur.

withstood the barbarian hordes to unite the British. His name was King Arthur and he was mortally wounded fighting his last battle, destined to be carried off, along with his knights, to sleep until Britain would be in need of him once more.

There have been various suggestions as to where his grave may be found, including Glastonbury Abbey in Somerset and Tintagel Castle in Cornwall. Many claim to have seen the

Glastonbury Abbey, Somerset, England. This has been a place of worship for over 1,000 years, and was an important centre of learning, rather like Oxford and Cambridge are today. With its links with Arthurian legend and with Joseph of Arimathea, who is reputed to have given up his own tomb for Christ to be buried in after the Crucifixion, Glastonbury has had a long and dramatic history. There is a legend that Joseph came to Glastonbury after the Crucifixion, where he set his staff into the ground, which broke into leaf and flower – now called the Glastonbury Thorn.

There is another legend, connected with Glastonbury, of a dark knight with red eyes, who is said to have destroyed all written references to the graves of King Arthur and his queen, Guinevere, but whose ghostly presence has long since departed. Today, and for many years, there have also been sightings of spectral monks, and visitors have heard the sounds of mysterious chanting; several people have reported seeing a white form haunting the abbey grounds, while other spectres include a mad monk, who wanders the orchard, also the dark spirit of a monk who was one of Henry VIII's spies; the ghost surveys the grounds, watching and waiting.

ghostly figures of Arthur and his knights riding through the skies, preparing to reappear once more.

But this is not the only legend of such a monarch. The Holy Roman Emperor, Frederick II, is believed to have died suddenly in 1250, but for years after, men appeared claiming to be him. Two imposters were ultimately executed, simply to prove that Frederick was indeed dead.

MOTHER RED CAP

Samuel Palmer, in his *History of St. Pancras*, recounts the story of Mother Red Cap, of Camden Town, London.

Jinney Bingham was the daughter of a Kentish Town brickmaker and a Scottish peddler. She accompanied her parents on their travels around the country, but on her 16th birthday fell in with a man called Gypsy George Coulter. By all accounts he was

OPPOSITE: Tintagel Castle, Cornwall – a fortress once used by King Arthur.

BELOW: The famous Camden Market. Camden Town was the home of Jinney Bingham and the site of her cottage in Camden High Street became the Mother Red Cap Inn, renamed the World's End.

something of a rogue and together they embarked on a career of stealing sheep.

GHOSTLY TALES & LEGENDS

BELOW: Camden High Street today.

OPPOSITE: The Old Bailey, where Gypsy George was sentenced to hang at Tyburn.

Gypsy George, after a spell spent in Newgate Prison, was eventually found guilty at the Old Bailey and was duly hung at Tyburn. Shortly afterwards, Jinney met a man called Darby, who inexplicably went missing, while around the same time her parents were called upon to face charges of witchcraft. It seems they had conspired to kill a girl and they were both hung for the crime. With her parents dead and Darby gone, Jinney then went to live with a man called Pitcher, but he, too, was destined to die, and the remains of his body were found crouched inside an oven. Jinney was tried for the murder but, on the strength of witness testimony, it was believed that Pitcher had hidden himself in the oven to escape Jinney's wicked tongue.

For a time, Jinney's life continued to be difficult until a homeless fugitive knocked upon her door and persuaded her to give him lodgings. After a while

192

he too died, and although it was believed he had been poisoned, there was no evidence to incriminate Jinney, although according to rumour prevalent at the time, it appears that the deceased had not been without money.

Jinney was now on her own, except for her huge black cat and occasional visits from Moll Cut-Purse, the notorious highwaywoman. The locals believed Jinney was a witch, and often consulted her as a fortune-teller and healer; but on one occasion, when a treatment went wrong, she was attacked by a mob of locals. Jinney was described as a tall woman, with a heavy, broad nose, thick eyebrows and sunken eyes. She also had a wrinkled forehead, a wide mouth, and an habitually sullen face. By now she had taken to wearing a red cap, and habitually wore a striped blanket around her shoulders, which had so many patches, that, from a distance, they resembled bats.

On the day of her death, numerous witnesses claimed to have seen the Devil himself go into her house to claim her soul. Indeed, her body was found that very morning beside the

fireplace. In front of her was a teapot containing herbs that had been made into a potion. When someone gave her cat some of the liquid, its hair fell out within two hours and it died soon afterwards. As for Mother Red Cap, her body was so stiff that the funeral director had to break her bones to get it into the coffin. It is believed that the Old Mother Red Cap Inn, built on the site of her cottage, is still haunted by her restless and tormented spirit.

THE ORIENT EXPRESS

In 1923 a man committed suicide on board the Orient Express, who had just stolen a package of diamonds from his employer, an Amsterdam diamond broker. He boarded the train, believing he had given the police the slip, but somehow got to know that police were waiting for him at the next station. Shortly after the train left Wurzburg, the man shot himself in one of the train's luxury compartments. From then on, anyone sleeping in that particular

THIS PAGE: Exterior and interior views of the Orient Express.

OPPOSITE: The Isle of Wight lies off the south coast of England.

compartment, as the train passes Wurtzburg, hears a sharp pistol shot and has the distinct feeling that they are not alone.

THE PHANTOM CITY

In 1969 a Dr White and his wife were driving towards the village of Niton on the Isle of Wight, that lies off the south coast of England. They began to see moving lights in the fields ahead, which they took to be people moving about in the darkness using torches. As they climbed a hill, they began to see the fields much more clearly, and instead of a handful of lights, they now saw what appeared to be a vast city lying beneath them. As they approached what appeared to be a farm track, it mysteriously changed into a city street, with buildings on either side.

They eventually reached a crossroads to the south of Newport, where the Hare and Hounds Inn is located. The inn was bathed in light and figures carrying torches appeared to be running across the road ahead of them. But as quickly as they had appeared, however, the lights and figures disappeared.

The couple decided to drive on towards their destination. They returned the same way in the early hours of the following day, but this time encountered nothing untoward.

There have been a number of explanations for what appears to be an incredibly elaborate manifestation. The couple believed that the man they had seen outside the inn looked rather like a Viking, while others suggest that what they had seen may have been a throwback to an ancient Roman camp. Others saw it, however, as a more sinister vision of the future, when cities would invade the land where once only fields and scattered houses had been.

Cynics dismissed the phenomenon simply as a mirage, in that the city of Portsmouth lay on the mainland, in close proximity across the water, and that the visions they had seen were the lights of the city reflected in the clouds. But it can never explain away the torch-bearing figures that ran in front of the couple's car that night.

Carisbrooke Castle, on the Isle of Wight, is one of the finest examples of a Norman castle. One of its most famous occupants was King Charles I, who was imprisoned here for ten months, before his execution at the culmination of the Civil War.

The castle was built on the site of earlier Roman and Saxon defences and, befitting its long and eventful history, has many ghostly tales to tell.

Elizabeth Ruffin, the young daughter of the Mayor of Newport, threw herself into Carisbrooke's deep well in 1632, and was tragically drowned, since when, many have reported seeing her face in its water. The castle also has a Grey Lady, who wears a long cloak and is accompanied by four dogs, while a young man in a brown jerkin is sometimes seen in the vicinity of the moat. Also witnessed is the ghost of a woman, wearing Victorian dress, who is followed by two shadowy dogs, while an apparition in a long coat has also been seen in broad daylight, accompanied by four small dogs.

CHAPTER SIX
GHOSTLY MESSAGES

*T*he First World War, remembered for its senseless slaughter of thousands of young men on the Western Front, has generated scores of ghostly tales, and many of these are in the archives of the Society for Psychical Research (SPR).

PREMONITIONS

Many of the tales take the form of ghostly warnings. On 6 November 1917, Mrs. Russell, whose husband was away fighting in France, and her son Richard, aged three-and-a-half, were sitting at home in England. She could not have known that her husband would be killed that same day, and that

LEFT: Professor Henry Sidgwick, an English philosopher, was one of a group of eminent thinkers who founded the Society for Psychical Research in 1882. Its headquarters are in London.

ABOVE & OPPOSITE: The horrors of the First World War produced many ghost stories.

she would not be officially informed of the fact for another ten days. Suddenly, the little boy sat bolt upright and proclaimed 'Daddy's dead.' Mrs. Russell tried to calm the boy, but he was insistent, repeating 'Dick knows he's dead.'

Up until then, Mrs. Russell had had no particular worries concerning the safety of her husband: after all, he had survived the war so far without a scratch. But at the very moment the child began to speak, her husband lay dying on the battlefield.

Mrs. Spearman was in India with her newborn child on the morning of 19 March 1917. She was the half-sister of Captain Eldred Bowyer-Bower, who was a 22-year-old pilot, and Mrs. Spearman would be but one of three people to receive a premonition that Eldred had just died in combat. This is what she had to say: 'I had a great feeling that I must turn around and did to see Eldred. He looked so happy and had that dear mischievous look. I was so glad to see him and told him I would put baby in a safer place, then we could talk. "Fancy coming out here," I said, turning round again, and I was just putting my hands out to give him a hug and a kiss, but Eldred had gone. I called and looked for him. I never saw him again.'

There were two other remarkable sightings of Eldred that same day. Mrs. Cecily Chater, the mother of Eldred's niece, who was then about three, suddenly came into her bedroom at 0915 on the morning of 19 March. The little girl said, 'Uncle Alley Boy is downstairs.' This was her nickname for her uncle. Her mother told her that he was in France, but the little girl was insistent that she had just seen him. Mrs. Chater forgot the incident, but was stunned when she discovered that it had occurred almost at the precise time that Eldred had been killed in France.

Eldred's mother was friendly with a Mrs. Watson, who was an elderly lady, but due to her infirmity she had not written to Eldred's mother for a year and a half. Out of the blue came a letter from Mrs. Watson, dated 19 March 1917, in which she said: 'Something tells me you are having great anxiety about Eldred. Will you let me know?'

When Eldred's mother received the letter she knew nothing of her son's death. She later spoke to Mrs. Watson, who told her how she had experienced a strong sense of dread that morning, and had been compelled to write the letter.

There is yet another remarkable story of a pilot in the First World War. Lieutenant David McConnell was just 18 when he had taken off on a training flight on 7 December 1918, after the hostilities had ceased. McConnell found himself flying in thick fog and crashed on landing at Tadcaster in England. His watch was broken in the crash and had stopped at precisely 1525. At exactly the same time at his home base at Scampton, his roommate, Lieutenant Larkin, saw McConnell, standing a few feet away from him. Larkin would later attest that this had happened some time between 1515 and 1530, but he did not know for hours afterwards that McConnell had in fact been killed.

Lady Charles Somerset first recounted this strange tale in 1827, concerning Lady Beresford, who habitually wore a black velvet ribbon around her wrist, that had been handed down through the family since the 18th century. Lady Beresford and her brother, Lord Tyrone, had made a pact in childhood that whoever died first would try to appear to the other.

Many years later, at 1600 one day, Lady Beresford had a strong premonition that her brother had just died, and soon afterwards her brother appeared to her, telling her she would die in her 47th year, and that she would bear her husband two daughters and a son. To prove that he was indeed dead, her brother touched his sister's wrist; from that point on, Lady Beresford wore a black ribbon tied around it.

The years passed and the children were born and to Lady Beresford's delight she was about to be 48. But she received a visit from an Irish clergyman, who told her that there had been a mistake and that she would in fact be celebrating her 47th birthday that day. Before midnight, Lady Beresford was dead.

Some believe she had broken a vow to her brother never to show her wrist, because she had spoken of the matter to her eldest son, who was then 12. When the ribbon was removed, the skin beneath was found to be puckered and the flesh and sinews shrunk.

THE WHITE LADY

The Hohenzollern dynasty ruled Prussia, and for generations had been plagued by the strange appearance of a lady in white. This only ever meant one thing: that there would be an imminent death or disaster in the family.

Lady of the Old Palace. I am sure you know what happens to those who see her.' With that the spectre disappeared.

Frederick William ignored the advice given to him and indeed the White Lady did appear, only a few days before Prince Louis of Prussia was killed fighting Napoleon's army.

It seems that the White Lady first appeared in around 1619, and the day after she was seen, the then ruler, John Sigismund, died. Her last reported sighting was in June 1914, when it was feared that Kaiser Wilhelm II would die. He did not, however, but that month Archduke Franz Ferdinand was

The most illustrious Hohenzollern was Frederick the Great, and he is reputed to have appeared in 1806 to his nephew, Frederick William. Prussia was then at war with France, pitted against the cunning and brilliant Napoleon Bonaparte. Frederick the Great's ghost warned his nephew to call off his attacks on Paris, telling him that 'you may expect to see someone who will not be welcome to you'. Frederick William pressed the ghost to tell him what this meant: 'I mean the White

assassinated, an event that triggered the First World War. The White Lady was correct: Germany lost the war and the German monarchy was swept aside forever.

ABOVE FAR LEFT: Hohenzollern Castle, the ancestral home of the Hohenzollern, including Frederick the Great and Kaiser Wilhelm II, the last German emperor.

ABOVE & PAGE 202 ABOVE: Kaiser Wilhelm II was possibly the last to see the White Lady before she finally disappeared.

LEFT: Frederick the Great.

her son, and her account is as follows: 'At that instant Jimmy stood right before me and said, "Momma, I never killed myself. My hands are as free from blood as when I was five years old." '

SUICIDE OR MURDER?

James Sutton was a lieutenant at the U.S. Naval Academy in Annapolis, Maryland. On 12 October 1907, Sutton had been to a dance and had had rather too much to drink, having picked a fight with some of his friends, from which he had emerged the worse for wear. He is reported to have returned to his room, where he kept a pair of pistols. The order was given for his arrest, but before this could happen, Sutton put a pistol to his head and pulled the trigger.

At precisely the same time in Portland, Oregon, Sutton's mother saw

Sutton's ghost then recounted to his mother what had happened, describing his wounds (remember that this was before his mother had been informed of his death). Tormented by what Mrs. Sutton claimed to have seen, the family had James's body exhumed from Arlington National Cemetery. The body was then examined, and wounds matching those of the ghost's description, which had not appeared in the doctor's report, were found.

This raised a number of questions, and although the case would never be officially reopened, there was genuine doubt as to whether or not James had in fact committed suicide, or that one of his colleagues had killed him.

GHOSTS OF THE WORLD

NORFOLK ISLAND GHOSTS

About 1,000 miles (1600km) to the north-east of Sydney, Australia, in the South Pacific, lies the former British penal colony of Norfolk Island. In 1856 it was settled by former inhabitants of the Pitcairn Islands, who were descendants of Fletcher Christian and *Bounty* mutineers, together with Tahitian women. Pitcairn Island was unable to support 200 inhabitants, and Queen Victoria offered them Norfolk Island, where the residents have often seen the ghosts of these mutineers.

Barney Duffy, a giant of an Irishman, was imprisoned on Norfolk Island, but he escaped and was pursued by British Redcoats before being finally captured. He had managed to stay

OPPOSITE: The ruins of Norfolk Island's New Gaol (Jail) was commenced in 1836 but was not completed until 1847.

RIGHT: Norfolk Island has a gruesome history, reflected in such place-names as Ghost Corner, Slaughter Bay, Cemetery Bay and Gallows Gate. The famous Bloody Bridge (right) was where a tyrannical overseer was killed and entombed during the bridge's construction.

hidden for seven years in a hollow pine, where he had lived like an animal, dressed in tattered rags. When he was captured, he cursed the soldiers, foretelling they would meet violent ends within a week of his death

Duffy was hanged for his many crimes. Two days later, the soldiers went fishing in the vicinity of Barney's hollow pine, and their battered bodies were found floating in the water shortly afterwards.

CHAPTER SEVEN
GHOSTLY PHENOMENA

*M*any people believe these phenomena to be actual sightings of individuals, having escaped their normal time, location or existence. In other words, they can be explained away as simple time slips. It is believed that windows frequently open in time, allowing brief moments for someone to view or experience something that has happened in another dimension.

This might well explain the fact that Vikings were seen on England's Isle of Wight in 1969, or that phantom towns and cities sometimes appear, and that soldiers can be seen forever fighting battles that once claimed their lives.

If we follow this line of thought to its conclusion, it may explain the phenomena connected with the Bermuda Triangle, where many believe inexplicable events have occurred.

THE DISAPPEARING 5TH BATTALION
A strange event took place during the Battle of Gallipoli, in Turkey, when 22 New Zealand soldiers saw what appeared to be a number of British soldiers, marching into a cloud.

During the First World War, the 5th Battalion of the Norfolk Regiment, from Sandringham, England, embarked for Gallipoli on 29 July 1915, preparing to make a strike against the Turks, who were allies of the Germans. What happened to the Sandringhams on the afternoon of 12 August 1915, during the disastrous Dardanelles campaign, and in the midst of their very first battle, no one knows. One minute the men were making a brave charge against the Turkish enemy – the next, they had disappeared, and their bodies were never found. Of the battalion of 257 men, no survivors were reported and none turned up later as prisoners-of-war. They had simply vanished.

Much later, in 1919, when the Graves Registration Unit arrived on the scene to recover bodies from hastily dug graves, only 122 of the missing men were found. What happened to the rest of them remains a mystery to this day.

THE BATTLE OF GETTYSBURG
Over the three days of the Battle of Gettysburg, during the American Civil War in 1863, some 8,000 men lost their lives. A bizarre incident, that cannot be dismissed as mere coincidence, took place in September 2003 on the battlefield at Gettysburg, in Pennsylvania. A man visiting the site heard odd noises. He asked if there was anybody there, and the reply, 'Grossy', came. The man asked where he was from, to which the ghostly voice replied 'Virginia'. When the witness checked the Civil War records, he found only a single match; it seems that Michael B Grossy was a Union soldier belonging to a Maryland regiment.

It transpired that Grossy had been shot in the head on 2 July 1863, and had died shortly after, near to the

OPPOSITE: The Battle of Gettysburg, fought 1–3 July 1863. Gettysburg's fallen dead (above), and its battlefield battery (below).

Wheatfield, where over 1,000 men had lost their lives.

UB65

The German submarine, UB65, was due to be launched in 1916, but things started to go wrong right from the beginning. A large, steel girder broke from its chains, crushing a worker, while another was badly injured and died two hours later. A little before the submarine's launch the engines were being tested and three men died in the engine-room, overcome by noxious fumes. On its maiden voyage, a man was washed overboard, then one of the

207

Canterbury Cathedral, England. The cathedral's history stretches back to AD 597, when St. Augustine, sent by Pope Gregory the Great as a missionary to Britain, established his seat (in Latin cathedra) in Canterbury. In 1170, the then archbishop, later to be St. Thomas à Becket, was murdered here and ever since, thousands of pilgrims – as famously told in Geoffrey Chaucer's Canterbury Tales – have been attracted to his shrine.

It is Simon Sudbury, however, another archbishop of Canterbury, who haunts the cathedral. Sudbury was also murdered, beheaded by Wat Tyler in 1381, who headed the Peasant's Revolt. Sudbury's ghost, which haunts the tower that bears his name, has a pale, grey-bearded face, even though his head was buried separately from his body. There is also the ghost of a monk, which walks the cloisters bearing a thoughtful expression on its face.

There is a passageway in the cathedral, known as the Dark Entry, which is said to be haunted by the ghost of Nell Cook, who was the servant of a canon. Legend has it that Nell, after discovering that her employer was having an affair, became thoroughly enraged and poisoned both the canon and his lover. Her punishment for the crime was to be buried alive beneath the Dark Entry, which her ghost still haunts on dark Friday evenings.

ballast tanks sprang a leak. Repairs took half a day, by the end of which, half of the test crew was dead.

When the submarine returned to port, it was loaded up with torpedoes, one of which exploded, killing the second officer. Sightings of apparitions began soon after this: just before the submarine was due to begin its first mission in August 1917, a crewman saw what he knew to be the dead officer, coming onboard. A second man had seen it too and was cowering in fright.

The German navy became concerned about the rumours flying around, and sent a senior officer to investigate; he was convinced that the crew was telling the truth. The submarine was put in dry dock in Belgium, where a Lutheran pastor carried out an exorcism.

The submarine completed its first two tours of duty without incident, largely because the captain had threatened the crew with severe punishment if ghosts were ever mentioned. When he was replaced, however, everything started up again.

In May 1918, off the coast of Spain, the ghost of the second officer was seen once more, and another sighting tipped a torpedo crewman over the line and into insanity, causing him to throw himself overboard.

BELOW: The submarine UB65 was plagued with problems prior to and after its launch, which resulted in many deaths. Ghostly sightings were subsequently made until, inexplicably, it blew up in 1918.

OPPOSITE: The legend of the Flying Dutchman *has inspired writers and composers down the ages. It was also the inspiration for the movie,* Pandora and the Flying Dutchman, *starring James Mason and Ava Gardner.*

An American submarine spotted the U-boat on 10 July 1918, situated a little to the south of the Irish coast. The Americans moved into the attack, but

before they could fire their torpedoes at the target the German submarine blew apart. When the Americans went to investigate, all that remained was smoke and debris, and every man belonging to the crew of 34 had perished.

THE FLYING DUTCHMAN

A far earlier nautical apparition dates back to the 17th century, and is probably the best known of all such ghost stories, having been immortalized in Wagner's opera. The legend of the *Flying Dutchman* has some basis in reality, however.

Captain Hendrick Vanderdecken left Amsterdam, in the Netherlands, bound for Batavia in the Dutch East Indies in 1680. As the vessel rounded the Cape of Good Hope, a major storm erupted, causing the ship to flounder. The entire crew perished, and as punishment for his arrogance in trying to beat the storm, the captain and his crew were doomed to continue sailing for eternity.

In 1835 a British ship was the first to encounter the ghostly *Flying Dutchman*. It was heading towards them in a storm, and the two ships seemed to be on a collision course; fortunately, the *Flying Dutchman*

The Colosseum, Rome. Known more correctly as the Flavian amphitheatre, this is the largest and most imposing building in Rome, even though it is a mere shadow of its former glory. It was begun between AD 70 and 72 by the Flavian Emperor Vespasian, and was opened by his son, Titus, in AD 80. Seating 50,000 spectators, some of the contests staged in the arena, which could even be flooded for mock sea battles, were between evenly-matched gladiators, but some were between people and wild animals, so it is no wonder that traces should remain of its cruel and violent past.

Visitors to the Colosseum at night have reported hearing the clash of swords, horses snorting, and the trundle of chariot wheels. There are also stories of a woman having been pulled back into the Colosseum when she tried to leave, and of another who experienced a timeslip, in which she was transported back to the time of the gladiatorial battles of ancient Rome.

suddenly vanished from sight. Later, in 1881, two crewmen of HMS *Bacchante* saw the ghostly vessel, and a man fell to his death from the rigging the following day.

The ghost ship came so close to the coast of South Africa in March 1939 that it could be seen by bathers on the beach. The last full sighting took place in 1942, when the *Flying Dutchman* was seen off the coast of Cape Town. Four people clearly saw it sail into Table Bay before it vanished from view.

USS HORNET

The eighth American naval vessel to bear the name USS *Hornet* had been involved in attacks on Tinian, Saipan, Iwo Jima, the Philippines, and Okinawa, winning nine battle stars for her service in the Second World War. She would hit the headlines again in 1969, when she recovered the Apollo 11 astronauts, returning from the moon. She was finally decommissioned in 1970 and was

later designated an historic landmark at the former naval air station in Alameda, California.

USS *Hornet* is believed to be the most haunted warship in the American navy, and has been host to televised paranormal programmes on several occasions. Footsteps and voices have been heard, ghostly shapes of sailors and officers have appeared and disappeared, strong winds have been felt in enclosed rooms, and radios and other equipment have turned themselves on and off. Even skeptics have admitted seeing officers in khakis descending ladders.

It is not surprising she has been host to so many manifestations, for although she was not the USS *Hornet* that was sunk during the Battle of the Santa Cruz Islands, in October 1942, at least 300 people died on her between 1943 and 1970 – some as a result of accidents, others of combat.

Foremost among the apparitions is the former captain, Admiral Joseph James Clark, who died in 1971. Clark was from Oklahoma and of Cherokee heritage, being the first Native American to graduate from the U.S. Naval Academy in Annapolis, Maryland, in 1917. He, together with the other ghosts on the vessel, is not malevolent, but rather playful and friendly.

THE PHANTOM CANOE

In another time and another place, an altogether different warship has been seen. On 31 May 1886, a group of tourists were travelling across Lake Tarawera in the North Island of New Zealand, in the same year that there had

been a substantial eruption of Mount Tarawera, which had claimed the lives of 150 people and buried a Maori village on the southern shore of the lake.

The tourists saw a large Maori canoe travelling parallel to their vessel. It was a large and powerful sea-going canoe, called a *waka*, which was manned by around 80 paddlers. When the tourists asked the local Maori elders about it, they were aghast, as such a vessel had never been seen on the lake before. The Maoris believed that a major disaster was about to befall, and they were correct, when 11 days later, the volcano claimed many Maori lives.

THE QUEEN MARY

The Cunard White Star Line ocean-going liner, the RMS *Queen Mary*, sailed the Atlantic route between 1936 and 1967, and she and the *Queen Elizabeth* dominated transatlantic passenger trade in the post-Second World War period. John Brown & Co., of Clydebank, Scotland, built her, and the *Queen Mary* took nearly six years to complete. During the Second World War, she served as a troop ship, but

The Queen Mary, *a much-haunted liner.*

LEFT & OPPOSITE: Once a great ocean-going liner, the Queen Mary is now a luxury hotel, berthed off Long Beach in California.

after 30 years of service had earned her rest and was converted into a luxurious hotel, lying off Long Beach, California; her 150 rooms were opened to guests in 1972.

Having seen so many people come and go and witnessed the dramas of their lives over the years, including passenger deaths, it is hardly surprising that she has several haunted hotspots on board. In the 1960s, the engine room, for example, was the place where a member of the crew was crushed to death by door 13, and where his ghost still appears. In another engine room, the ghosts of stowaways who died during the voyage can also sometimes be seen, and the pool is haunted by two children. There is the occasional smell of seasick – also a supposed vortex, through which it is possible to pass into another dimension. This is understood to lie directly beneath a revolving door, that was once used as the entranceway to the pool.

Pompeii, now a UNESCO World Heritage Site, is a ruined Roman city, situated near modern Naples, in Campania, Italy. Pompeii, along with the city of Herculaneum, was destroyed and buried beneath many layers of ash and pumice during the catastrophic eruption of the supposedly extinct volcano, Mount Vesuvius, that lasted for two days in August, AD 79. The city was lost for nearly 1700 years before it was accidentally rediscovered in 1748, since when excavations have continued to provide fascinating insights into the nature of city life at the height of the Roman Empire.

As one might expect, in a place where such violence has occurred, in which thousands were buried alive, paranormal phenomena have been experienced. People claim to have heard screams, seen shadowy figures, and smelt the tang of sulphur in the air.

Others have heard the cries of dying men near the bows of the ship; on 2 October 1942, the *Queen Mary* collided with the British light cruiser, HMS *Curacao*, when 338 lives were lost. None of the survivors could be rescued because the *Queen Mary* had been ordered not to stop, or even slow down, for fear it would be attacked by U-boats.

BACHELORS GROVE CEMETERY, MIDLOTHIAN, ILLINOIS

The people of Chicago have been burying their dead at Bachelors Grove Cemetery since 1834, said to be the most haunted graveyard in the world. Legend has it that the cemetery was named after the many German bachelor immigrants, who died during the construction of the 62.5-mile (101-km) Illinois & Michigan Canal, from 1836 until its completion in 1848. In 1984, the canal was designated the first National Heritage Corridor by the U.S. Congress.

Bachelors Grove also has close associations with Chicago gangland killings. There is a small lagoon, surrounding the cemetery, which was used as a dumping ground for murdered victims of the mob during the days of Prohibition. For some time, bodies

have been routinely popping up out of the water.

The cemetery is home to many strange manifestations and apparitions, one of which is the White Lady, also known as the Madonna of Bachelors Grove. She appears when there is a full moon, holding a baby in her arms.

Some have seen blue lights and orbs, while others have witnessed ghostly automobiles similar to the gangster

BELOW: Bachelors Grove, named after the many German bachelor immigrants, who worked and died there during the construction of the Illinois & Michigan Canal.

OPPOSITE: The home of Ronald De Feo Jr. It was De Feo's horrendous crime, in which he murdered his entire family in 1974, that inspired the novel, The Amityville Horror, *published in 1977.*

vehicles of the 1940s. The *Chicago Sun Times* featured a photograph, taken in the late 1980s or early 1990s, of an apparition of a woman, sitting on a grave, while beside the path leading to the cemetery, a white farmhouse spontaneously appeared on a number of occasions in the 1950s. In the 1970s, a pair of forest rangers saw the ghost of a 1870s farmer, who had fallen into the water of the lagoon with his horse while ploughing.

AMITYVILLE, SUFFOLK COUNTY, NEW YORK

Amityville, the setting for the novel *The Amityville Horror*, published in 1977, would later become the basis of a number of movies, made between 1979 and 2005. Although it was a work of fiction, the novel was in fact based on a real murder case, that took place in November 1974, when Ronald De Feo Jr. murdered both of his parents, his two brothers and two sisters.

The scene of the crime was 112 Ocean Avenue, and during his trial De

GHOSTLY PHENOMENA

Feo claimed to have heard voices, ordering him to murder his family. The court rejected his plea of insanity and gave him six consecutive life sentences.

George and Kathy Lutz bought the house at a knockdown price in December 1975, due to its terrible associations, but the family lived there for barely a month, claiming to have been driven out by paranormal phenomena. A massive police investigation followed, in which

Coroner's office employees removing bodies from 112 Ocean Drive, Amityville. Robert De Feo Jr. admitted murdering his family, but claimed he had heard voices telling him to do it.

parapsychologists and the Roman Catholic Church were also involved. There were even rumours that the land on which the house stood had been contaminated by an evil force.

The real truth, however, may have been more to do with money than manifestations, in that it was the Lutz family itself which contacted the writer, Jay Anson, asking him to write a book describing their experiences. He, in turn, produced a highly sensationalized account, with all the right ingredients of a best-seller, including demons, plagues of flies and mass murder.

As for De Feo, he too was probably motivated by money, there being the strong possibility that if only he could get away with the crime he would collect the vast insurance, taken out on the lives of his parents.

BLACK AGGIE

General Felix Angus died in 1925, having been the publisher of the Baltimore *American*. He was buried in the Pikeville Druid Ridge Cemetery, close to Baltimore in Maryland. Sitting on top of his grave was a black sculpture of a mourning figure, which in daylight was that of a beautiful angel; but as darkness fell, however, the statue's eyes began to glow. It has been dubbed 'Black Aggie', and legend has it that the ghosts of the cemetery gather around her at midnight, and that any living person seeing them will be struck blind. No grass grows beneath her shadow, and a pregnant woman is sure to miscarry should Black Aggie's shadow fall upon her.

Members of a local college took it upon themselves to make Black Aggie a part of an initiation rite. The unlucky candidate was obliged to spend the night in her company, but the practice abruptly stopped when one of the candidates was discovered to have died of fright.

Black Aggie became so notorious that the Angus family decided it would have to intervene; she was removed from the grave and donated to the Smithsonian Institution in 1967. Rumour has it that even the Smithsonian avoids putting her on show, for fear that her curse will fall upon its visitors.

MISTAKEN FOR DEAD

In 1878, the young daughter of D.J. Demarest, a grocer from Patterson, New Jersey, suddenly died, and the body was prepared for burial the following week. Demarest, who had been weeping and praying beside the coffin, suddenly became so overcome by grief and exhaustion, that he slumped into an armchair, falling into a deep sleep.

He awoke to see what he thought was an apparition of his daughter, standing in the doorway, clad in her shroud. She walked across to her father, sat in his lap, and put her arms around his neck. All of a sudden, however, the girl went limp and her father tried in vain to raise her up. In desperation, Demarest called a doctor, who confirmed that the girl had been in a coma, but that this time she was well and truly dead. It is believed that Demarest brought the funeral forward and the girl was buried that very day.

CORDER'S SKULL

On 11 August 1828, at Bury St. Edmunds in Suffolk, England, William Corder was hanged for an infamous murder at the Red Barn. Although there is considerable speculation as to whether or not Corder was indeed the murderer, he was convicted of shooting Maria Marten dead. According to the common practice of the day, Corder's body was sent to a medical school for dissection.

Somewhat bizarrely, his skin was tanned, and was used in the leather binding of a book containing details of his trial. His skeleton continued to be used to teach anatomy and much later, a Dr. Kilner stole Corder's skull and replaced it with another. Kilner polished up Corder's skull and placed it as a decoration in his drawing room.

From that moment on, anyone entering the room began to feel decidedly uncomfortable. Strange noises were also heard, hammering was common, doors opened and closed of their own accord, and Kilner's servants saw a man dressed in an old-fashioned manner.

Kilner was unconvinced that these goings-on had occurred at all, but was soon to change his mind. Lying in bed one night, he was awoken by a loud noise, causing him to leap from his bed and go to investigate. He arrived

RIGHT: The polished skull of William Corder haunted those who owned it, bringing misfortune in its wake.

OPPOSITE: The Chase Vault, in which coffins moved around by themselves.

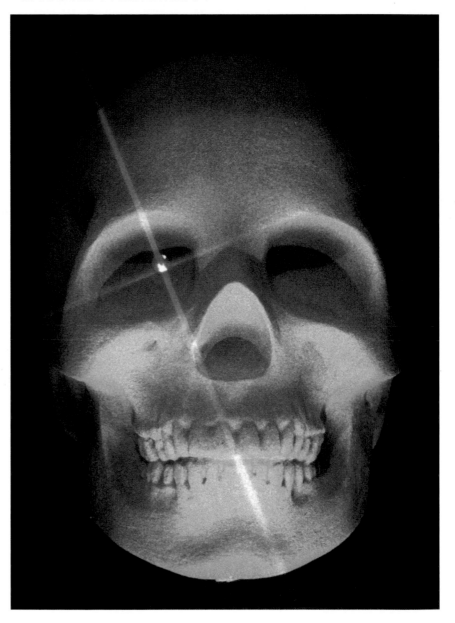

226

downstairs in time to see a white hand opening the drawing-room door, but as he approached, the door was literally blown off its hinges. Undaunted, the doctor strode into the drawing room, to be met by a blast of ice-cold air. His candle went out, and Kilner fumbled for a match; in the flickering light, he saw the skull lying on the floor, grinning up at him, and the fragments of the box, in which by now the skull was kept, were scattered across the room.

Kilner decided to dispose of the skull: his first thought was to return it to the place from which he had stolen it, but having already polished it up, its theft would have been immediately obvious. Instead, he decided to give the skull as a gift to a retired prison commissioner, F.C. Hopkins. Hopkins already had a somewhat macabre possession, in that he had bought the old Bury St. Edmunds jail, in which Corder had been executed.

Hopkins was delighted with the gift, but on his way home tripped and the skull rolled out of the handkerchief in which it was wrapped, causing a woman who saw it to promptly faint. Shortly afterwards, both Kilner and Hopkins were

declared bankrupt, having presumably been afflicted by the evil influence of the skull. It was ultimately Hopkins who decided to put an end to the matter forever; he selected a graveyard in which to bury the skull, and the curse was broken the moment it touched the consecrated ground.

THE CHASE VAULT

Not far from Bridgetown, the capital of Barbados, is a graveyard known as Christ Church, in which there is an enormous edifice known as the Chase Vault. It was originally built for the Chase family, but others were also interred in it. The first coffin to be

St. Michael's Mount, an island lying in
Mount's Bay, off the coast of Marazion,
Penzance, Cornwall, is accessible by boat,
but it can also be reached at low tide, by
walking to it across the sands. It is a
truly magical place, with a church, a
medieval castle (the home of the St. Aubyn
family for over 300 years), an exotic
garden clinging to its steep flanks, and an
historic harbour.

It goes without saying that the Mount
has its fair share of ghostly phenomena.
There is the ghost of a Grey Lady, that has
been seen running down the castle's Long
Passage and disappearing through the
window at the end. The ghost, often heard
and seen by the castle's residents, is
thought to be that of a maid who once
worked at the castle. Having given birth to
a child, she was jilted by her lover at the
altar, leading her to throw herself through
the window onto the rocky slopes below.

There is another more mischievous
presence, that rattles and turns doorknobs,
and hides objects away that turn up many
days later.

placed in the vault, in July 1807, contained the body of Thomasina Goddard, joined the following year by that of two-year-old Mary Ann Chase, and in 1812 by that of Mary Ann's older sister, Dorcas. In the same year, the body of the girls' father, Thomas Chase, was also interred.

Thomas Chase had an appalling reputation and was hated by the islanders, but there was the rumour that, because of his cruelty, Dorcas had starved herself to death. When Thomas Chase's coffin was brought into the chamber, it was discovered that the other coffins had changed position, and that Mary Ann's coffin had moved to the other side of the vault. The natural assumption was that someone had broken in, intent on robbery; this could not have been the case, however, because the cement, used to hold the entrance slab in place, had not been disturbed.

The coffins were repositioned and the vault was resealed. On 25 September 1816, the vault was opened again, this time to receive the body of Charles Brewster Ames. Once again it was discovered that the coffins had been moved around, including the lead coffin of Thomas Chase himself, which

had taken eight men to heave it into the vault.

Charles Ames's father, Samuel, joined his son a couple of months later, having been originally buried elsewhere. The ritual of chipping away the cement took place once more, and once the funeral party was inside it was immediately obvious that the coffins had been thrown around. Four of the five coffins had been made of lead and these were undamaged though in the wrong position, but Thomasina's coffin, that was made of wood, was badly damaged. In spite of a thorough investigation, no clear idea emerged as to how or why this was happening.

The vault was opened up again in July 1819. This time, the coffins of the children were placed on top of the larger ones, while the wooden coffin was propped up against the wall.

Lord Combermere, the governor of the island, came in person to investigate the situation. He decided to have sand sprinkled onto the floor of the vault, which would show up the footprints. of anyone entering it. He personally supervised the closing of the vault, pressing his seal into the wet cement.

In April 1820 the governor ordered the vault be opened again. Once again,

all the coffins were in disarray, with the exception of the wooden one, but there were no footprints in the sand. The governor was both angry and perplexed and ordered that the coffins be taken out and buried elsewhere. The Chase vault remained empty from that point on.

Some have pointed the finger of blame at Dorcas Chase, a suicide and therefore a restless spirit, while others hold that the ghost of Thomas Chase, being a man of evil reputation in life and, perhaps, even more malevolent in death, was responsible for the events.

FACES IN THE WATER

In December 1924 the oil tanker, SS *Watertown*, was heading towards the Panama Canal from the Pacific coast. Meanwhile, James Courtney and Thomas Meehan were busy at work cleaning out one of the cargo tanks. Fumes overcame them, however, and according to tradition, their bodies were buried at sea. Strange happenings began the very next day, when crew members reported seeing the faces of the dead men in the water, following in the wake of the ship.

The faces followed the ship for several days, and the tanker made it

The Panama Canal. Two men lost their lives on board the SS Watertown, *as it headed for the Panama Canal in 1924. They were buried at sea and the crew later saw the dead men's faces in the water.*

through the Panama Canal and reached New Orleans. At the port, an official of the city's service company gave Captain Tracy a roll of film, in the hope that he would be able to photograph the faces. In fact, six photographs were taken, five of which showed nothing of interest, while the sixth showed the faces very clearly.

By the time any real investigation was made into the matter, ten years had elapsed, by which stage the vessel's first mate had died and so had the official in New Orleans. It was also proving difficult to trace any of the crew members, including the captain.

What is clear is that the company had used a detective agency to check the authenticity of the photograph and that Captain Tracy and his assistant engineer had sworn that it was genuine. Unfortunately, the original negatives of the photographs had been lost, and it was never explained why only one photograph showed the faces, when the other five did not.

231

The coast of Calabria, Italy. Calabria occupies the toe of the 'boot' of Italy, being a narrow peninsula extending out into the Mediterranean Sea. It has the Tyrrhenian Sea to the west and the Ionian Sea and the Gulf of Taranto to the east.

A strange phenomenon has been experienced in the mountains of Calabria, where people have reported seeing a white light glowing in the night. Some say they have seen a pale woman, wearing a white dress, who walks around for a minute or so, before disappearing around midnight.

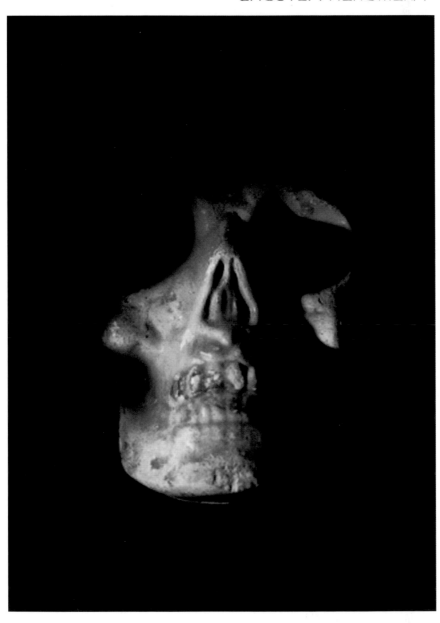

THE SCREAMING SKULL OF BETTISCOMBE MANOR

The strange case of Corder's Skull (page 225) is not unique, there having been other such manifestations in Britain, some of them equally perplexing. Perhaps the most famous is the phenomenon of the Screaming Skull of Bettiscombe Manor, where, it seems, the skull objects to being moved, screaming loudly if an attempt is made to bury it.

Legend has it that the skull belonged to a black servant, who on his deathbed declared that he would not rest until his remains had been returned to Africa. In fact the body was buried in a local graveyard, which became so bedevilled by the sound of screaming, that it was decided to dig up the remains of the corpse and bury it under the manor house. This ritual was performed several times and on each occasion resulted in screaming that lasted for

LEFT: Bettiscombe Manor's famous skull was said to scream its objections whenever there was talk of reburying it.

OPPOSITE & PAGES 236–237: The Isle of Skye, where phantom Highlanders were seen in 1956.

weeks on end. Over the years, most of the skeleton had been left underground, apart from the skull.

For many years, the skull remained silent, screaming only when there was talk of reburying it. It is also said that just before the outbreak of the First World War, the skull began to drip blood. By all accounts the skull is still somewhere in the house, but it is far more likely that it is not the same one, being another taken from a prehistoric burial site.

ANCIENT BATTLES

Soldiers go to battle, hopefully to return, but for some the fighting never seems to stop, even in death. This example of a spectral battle in Roman times is rather different, however, in that it is a look into the future rather than the past.

The local people began to report hearing the sounds of a battle being fought on a plain in Campania, and the marks of horses' hooves and other evidence of war were clearly seen imprinted in the ground. Witnesses believed it was a battle between evil spirits, when in fact it was a battle that had yet to be fought. Shortly after, a real battle occurred on the very spot.

Culloden, the last battle to be fought in mainland Britain, occurred on 16 April 1746. It was the final clash of the Jacobite Rising, that began in 1745, between the Jacobites, most of them Highland Scots, and the Hanoverians, the Jacobite cause having been to restore the House of Stuart (Stewart in Scotland) to the throne of England. The battle was bloody but was over and done with in an hour. It resulted in the slaughter of the Young Pretender, Bonnie Prince Charlie and his Highlanders by the Duke of Cumberland, the younger son of the Hanoverian sovereign, King George II.

People claim to see phantom armies locked in combat to this day, some of them clearly wearing tartans, while on the battlefield, a dark-haired Highlander, wearing the red Stewart tartan, has been seen at rest, sitting at the top of a stone cairn.

Highlanders of the same period were also seen in 1956, this time on the Isle of Skye in the Cuillin Hills. Two students were awoken at 0400 on a November morning to see exhausted Highlanders walking past.

In Croatia, in 1888, witnesses watched an enormous army of foot soldiers, led by a general with a flaming sword, marching across the sky. Others began to flock to Verasdin in the hope that they would see the vision for themselves and were rewarded by at least two more performances, some lasting for several hours.

PHANTOM FIRE

In June 1857, when the British were in India, two Bengali cavalrymen murdered their officer and his family before setting fire to their house. For several years afterwards, a chilling phenomenon was witnessed, confirmed by several British Army officers.

Buildings that had been constructed on the site of the tragedy began to feel hot in the middle of the night and there were flickering lights that suggested fire. On one occasion, in 1917, this occurred on four consecutive nights, and witnesses saw strangely dressed figures moving around. The officers thought it was a throwback to a past event, but on closer investigation found it to be a ghostly repeat of what had happened 60 years before.

SHADES OF AL CAPONE

Many of the places associated with the St. Valentine's Day Massacre and Al Capone (see also page 83) have

disappeared over the years, including the warehouse site on North Clark Street, where the massacre took place in 1929. Some will recall seeing

ABOVE: Al Capone, who died of natural causes on Alcratraz.

OPPOSITE: Today Chicago is a very different city, compared with the way it was in the 1920s and 1930s,

photographs of the bodies in the newspapers, and for some time the warehouse became something of a tourist attraction. In 1967, however, the building was demolished and a Canadian businessman bought the bullet-pocked bricks, using them to build a wall in the men's lavatory of his nightclub in 1972. When he closed the nightclub down, he placed the 417 bricks into storage before deciding to sell them for $1,000 apiece. The people who bought the bricks could not have known that, by doing so, they faced divorce, illness, financial ruin or death.

To this day, it is said that dogs howl when they approach the site, possibly sensing a malevolent spirit, while others claim to have heard the sounds of gunfire and people screaming.

LEFT: The S-M-C Cartage Company, at 2122 North Clark St, Chicago, was the site of the St. Valentine's Day Massacre on 14 February 1929. The building was demolished in 1967 and its bricks sold off for $1,000 each; anyone buying them, however, also bought bad luck.

RIGHT: The aftermath of the St. Valentine's Day Massacre. That day, six members of the O'Banion-Moran gang were trapped inside a garage, where they were waiting for an illegal consignment of alcohol. A Cadillac arrived instead, carrying three men dressed as policemen, who lined the six gangsters and a garage mechanic, up against a wall. The two civilians then entered and with sub-machine guns, mowed all seven down. Although Al Capone was assumed to be the instigator, no one was actually punished for the crime.

CHAPTER EIGHT
POLTERGEISTS

*T*he word poltergeist is German for 'noisy ghost', and what typifies poltergeist activity is the movement or throwing about of objects. Many such cases appear to involve a living individual that becomes part of the haunting against their will, so that they can almost be described as haunted people. The cases are often extraordinary and many instances of this strange phenomenon have occurred throughout the world.

ESTHER COX
Such a victim lived in Amherst, Nova Scotia. The year was 1878 and Esther

RIGHT: The case of the Enfield Poltergeist is one of the most famous in recent times. It revolved around 11-year-old Janet Harper, when activities such as knockings, moving furniture, and Janet being physically thrown from her bed, occurred in North London in 1977–78.

OPPOSITE: Here, covers are pulled back and the curtain moves as Janet lies asleep.

Cox was 19, living in a small rented house with her married sister, Olive Teed, Olive's husband, Daniel, and their two young children. The crowded little cottage was also home to Esther's siblings, Jennie and William, as well as to Daniel's brother John.

Suddenly, horror struck, but it was not of the paranormal kind. Esther was nearly raped by an acquaintance called Bob MacNeal, and although she escaped with minor injuries, the violence seemed to trigger what was about to happen next.

The family began to hear noises, coming from the room where Esther slept with her young sister, Jennie, and Esther awoke one morning to find that her arms and face were swollen. The source of the noise could not be found but, in the meantime, Esther's swelling subsided, only to reappear as bad as ever a few days later. Then an unseen hand began to tear the covers off the bed, objects were thrown around the room, and a message was found scrawled on the wall: 'Esther Cox you are mine to kill'.

Many believed Esther was causing the disturbances herself, but in truth she was terrified and had begun to feel thoroughly ill. She was sent to live elsewhere, when the poltergeist activity in the Teed home came to an abrupt halt, only to start up again when Esther returned. Matches were now being lit and dropped everywhere, starting small fires around the house. Then a spirit, calling itself Bob, began to communicate with Esther.

Daniel Teed ordered the tormented girl out of the house. She was able to get a job in a restaurant, only for the poltergeist to follow her there, and she eventually became homeless. Esther was later imprisoned for arson, when a barn was burned down, and no one believed her when she claimed that the poltergeist had caused the fire. After her release from prison, the poltergeist activity began to fade, eventually ceasing altogether.

POLTERGEISTS

THE BELL WITCH PHENOMENON

Back in 1817, in Robertson, Tennessee, John and Lucy Bell were living on a farm with their nine children. They began, first of all, to hear noises and scratching, then covers were pulled off the beds and furniture and other objects started to be thrown around.

Central to the activity seemed to be one of the children, Elizabeth. She and her brother, Richard, felt their hair being pulled, while on another occasion, the family and a neighbour witnessed Elizabeth being slapped around the face.

John Bell then began to get ill: his tongue swelled and the poltergeist, which now spoke, told him he would be tormented for the rest of his life. In desperation, Elizabeth was forced to be sick, in the belief that she harboured the spirit inside her body; she produced pins and needles.

After several years of intense suffering, his face by now distorted with pain, John Bell died on 20 December 1820. After his death the poltergeist activity began to subside and the last words uttered were, 'I will be gone for seven years'.

Some believe this was not in fact a poltergeist phenomenon, and that Elizabeth herself had somehow staged the events, to the extent, perhaps, even of poisoning her own father. Skeptics, however, suggest there may have been another root cause, such as an incestuous relationship between father and daughter.

THE DRUNKEN POLTERGEIST

Leon Dénizarth Hippolyte Rivail, a Paris intellectual, was the investigator of a strange case of a poltergeist haunting on the Rue des Noyers in 1860. It was a particularly bad-tempered and malevolent spirit, called St. Louis, which went about smashing windows and objects in the house, causing the family to flee.

Rivail made contact with the poltergeist through a medium, and it explained that it had died about 60 years before and was now operating through a maidservant. The poltergeist claimed to be taking its revenge on the occupants of the house, because it had been mocked for its drunkenness by them when it was still alive.

POLTERGEISTS AND PUBERTY

In March 1850, the Reverend E. Phelps, a man fascinated by the paranormal, held a séance at his home in Stratford, Connecticut. After the séance, the Phelps family went to church, but when they returned furniture had been moved around and cushions and pillows had been moulded to resemble human figures.

The poltergeist seemed to have two centres of focus. Reverend Phelps had a son, Harry, who was 12-years-old, and a daughter, Anna, aged 16, and, significantly, they were both going through puberty. The activity continued: stones were thrown, objects were smashed, and Anna was physically attacked. Then, when the family left the home for good, it stopped as abruptly as it had begun.

GUARDIAN OF THE TREASURE

Another bizarre case took place in Burma in 1928. In his book, *Trials in Burma,* Maurice Collis wrote of seeing the ghost of an old Arkanese woman. He had been working late into the evening with a colleague, when they both felt a tremor, almost as if a slight earthquake had momentarily rocked the building. Suddenly they were confronted by a woman, standing outside on the verandah. She did not speak, but disappeared the way she had

Brasilia, Brazil. Here, in 1960, a couple driving home from their wedding were mysteriously showered with stones.

come, vanishing where there was no place of exit.

Collis was shaken by the incident and the locals confirmed that a female ghost had been bound to the building by the old kings of Burma to guard their treasure, and that the woman had been buried alive so that her spirit remained trapped. When Collis asked why the house had been shaken, he was told that the ghost wished to attract his attention, and that the house had not in fact been shaken, but that it was his own mind that had moved.

SHOWERS OF STONES

Here are two cases from Brazil, separated from one another by only five years. The first took place in the capital, Brasilia, in 1960. On the night

of 18–19 September, a couple who had just got married were driving along the main road to Belo Horizonte, accompanied by their parents and a distinguished Brazilian doctor, Olavo Trindade. The road was clear and they had yet to reach the outskirts of the capital, when the car suddenly began to overheat. They stopped, and as they got out, stones began to fly at them from all directions, to which the driver, more in panic, responded by firing his pistol four times into the darkness.

The doctor collected up some of the stones and they got back into the car. They then went to show the stones to the police, offering to take them to the spot where the incident had occurred. This time, when the barrage of stones began, the driver found his gun had jammed. The police swept the area with their torches, but there was no one to be seen. They drove off again, under a bombardment of stones, and this time sand started to blow into the car.

Suddenly the driver sensed that someone was trying to open the car door, and despite struggling with the handle, the door opened and closed several times and the driver saw a vague form outside. When they escaped the area, not only had the driver's gun

unjammed, but there was also not a single scratch upon the car.

A FATAL CASE

In São Paulo, Maria José Ferreira was killed by a poltergeist. It was December 1965 and the poltergeist attacked Maria at her home in Jabuticabal, biting her, slapping her, and setting her clothes on fire. It even attempted to suffocate her in her sleep by putting objects over her nose and mouth.

One day, Maria ingested an insect repellant, but whether or not she was driven mad by the attacks and took poison herself, or it was the poltergeist that was responsible for her death, no one knows. She was only 13 when she died.

São Paulo, Brazil. Here in 1965, a poltergeist seems to have driven Maria José Ferreira to her death.

THE EXORCIST

The movie of the book, *The Exorcist,* was the first horror blockbuster, and although essentially a work of fiction, it was based on a real case.

The real-life subject was in fact a boy, rather than a girl. His name was Douglas Deen, he was 14, and he was living in a suburb of Washington, DC in 1949. Strange noises were heard, coming from his room, and his parents called in a rodent exterminator. Nothing unusual was found, however, and the noises continued.

The poltergeist activity gradually increased in intensity: furniture rocked, pictures fell off the walls, and Douglas's bed trembled and shook all night. Once they had spent a night in the house, skeptical neighbours had their views radically changed, which made it even more plain that drastic action was necessary.

The family then called in the Reverend Winston, who though also skeptical, agreed to spend the night in Douglas's room. He describes how Douglas's bed began to shake, and how he heard scratching and scraping coming from the walls. The clergyman flicked on the light, but there was nothing to be seen. He asked the boy

to get out of bed and sit in an
armchair, which immediately began to
move around the room before rocking
violently back and forth, tipping
Douglas onto the floor. The Reverend
tried to get Douglas to sleep on the
floor and gave him a pillow and a
blanket. But once again, Douglas was
thrown around the room.

Perplexed, the clergyman could offer
no explanation, and in desperation a
Roman Catholic priest was summoned
to perform an exorcism. Over a period
of two months, the priest repeated the
exorcism 30 times, and every time the
boy screamed and trembled, shouting
in a voice that was not his own. Finally,
in May 1949, the ritual was performed
once more, and this time brought no
violent reaction came from the boy. The
poltergeist activity appeared to have
ceased at last.

INDEX

A

Aetna Springs, California 50
Alamo, San Antonio, Texas 131–132
Alcatraz, St. Francisco 83, 85, 125–127
American Civil War 47, 60, 62, 63, 64, 127
American Revolution 58
Angus, General Felix 225
Appomattox Courthouse, Virginia 62
Arthur's Seat, Edinburgh, Scotland 101
Arundel Castle, England 154–155
Avebury, England 16–17

B

Balcarres, Lord 103
Barguest 165
Barrow, Clyde 76–77
Beaulieu, Hampshire, England 156–157
Becket, Thomas à 149, 209
Bedlam (see Bethlem Royal Hospital, London)
Beltane 103
Bentham, Jeremy 64, 68
Beresford, Lady 25, 200
Bermuda Triangle 206
Bern, Paul 80, 81, 82
Bethlem Royal Hospital, London 133–134
Bigod, Hugh 162
Bingham, Jinney 191, 192, 193
Black Dog of Bungay 161
Black Dog of Newgate 145
Black Shuck 158, 162, 164
Blackwall Tunnel, London 35–37
Blickling Hall, Norfolk 134–135
Blythburgh Church, Suffolk, England 164
Boleyn, Anne 15, 57, 134, 135, 149, 150
Boleyn, George 150
Bolingbroke Castle, Lincolnshire, England 171

Bolton Abbey, Yorkshire England 114–115
Booth, John Wilkes 47, 61
Borden, Lizzie 64
Borley Rectory, Essex, England 40–43, 68
Bowie, Jim 131, 132
Brandolini, Count 119, 122 119
Brisbane Arcade, Australia 100
Brisbane City Hall, Australia 101
British Museum, London 37, 38, 39
Brown Lady of Raynham, Norfolk, England 19
Brunel, Isambard Kingdom 36
Brynner, Yul 92
Buckingham Palace, London 135–136
Bull, Reverend Henry D.E. 40, 42
Bull, Henry Jr. 42, 43
Bulwer-Lytton, Sir Edward 72
Burr, Aaron 58–60

C

Cabot, Sebastian 36
Calton Hill, Edinburgh, Scotland 101
Cape Hatteras, North Carolina 60
Capone, Al 83–85, 125, 238–241
Carluccio's Tivoli Gardens Restaurant, Las Vegas 92
Cases of Hauntings
  Aaron Burr 58–60
  Abraham Lincoln 46, 47, 60–61, 62
  African Mask, The 39
  Alamo, The (Mission of San Antonio de Valero, San Antonio, Texas) 131–132
  Al Capone 83–85, 125, 238–241
  Alcatraz, San Francisco, California 83, 85, 125–127
  Amityville, Suffolk County, New York 223–225
  Ancient Battles 235, 238

Angels of Mons, The 176
Anne Frank House, Amsterdam, Netherlands 66–67
  Arundel Castle, England 154–155
  Avebury, England 16–17
  Bachelors Grove Cemetery, Midlothian, Illinois 222–223
  Bank of England, London 132
  Battle of Gettysburg 206–207
  Beaulieu, Hampshire, England 156–157
  Bedlam, London 133–134
  Bell Witch Phenomenon 25, 244
  Berlin, Germany 116
  Blackwall Tunnel, London 35–37
  Black Aggie 225
  Blickling Hall, Norfolk, England 134–135
  Bolton Abbey, Yorkshire, England 114–115
  Bonnie and Clyde 76–77
  Borley Rectory 40–43, 68
  Brisbane, Queensland, Australia 100–101
  Buckingham Palace, London 135–136
  Building 20, Fort McNair 46–47
  Caerphilly Castle, Wales 178
  Calabria, Italy 232–233
  Carisbrooke Castle, Isle of Wight, England 196–197
  Carole Lombard 82–83
  Castle Brando, nr. Venice, Italy 119, 122
  Chase Vault, The 227, 230
  Cheyne Walk, Chelsea, London 136–138
  Cleopatra's Needle, London 138–139
  Colosseum, Rome 212–213
  Corder's Skull 225–227, 234
  Disappearing 5th Battalion 206
  Drunken Poltergeist 244

Durham Castle, England 32–33
Dylan Thomas 85–86
Edinburgh, Scotland 101, 102, 103, 105, 108
Eiffel Tower, Paris, France 30–31
Elvis Presley 15, 89–91
Enfield Poltergeist 242, 243
Esther Cox 242–243
Exeter Cathedral, England 22–23
Exhibit 22542 37–38
Exorcist, The 248–249
Faces in the Water 230–231
Fatal Case, A 246
Flight 401 94
Flying Dutchman, The 211, 215
Fort Erie, Ontario, Canada 96
Ghosts of Versailles 117, 119
Glastonbury Abbey, Somerset, England 186, 188–189
Green Lady, Banffshire Scotland 176–177
Guardian of the Treasure 244–245
Hampton Court Palace, England 139–140
Harry Price 68
Harvard University, Cambridge, Massachusetts 52–53
Hatfield House, Hertfordshire, England 12–13
Holyrood House, Palace of 103, 104–105
Houdini 74–76
Hydesville Rappings 43–46
Imogen: A Victorian Ghost Story 34–35
James Dean 86, 88
James Sutton 202–203
Jean Harlow 80–82
Jeremy Bentham 64, 68
Jesse James 62–64
Katebit 39

King Arthur 186, 189, 191
King Family 69–70
Knebworth House, Hertfordshire, England 72
Krakow, Poland 108
Lady Mary Howard 54–58
La Llorna 24, 182, 185, 186
Liberace 92–93
Lizzie Borden 64
Lon Chaney 79–80
London Bridge, Re-erected in Arizona 122–123
Manhattan, New York City 123–125
Marilyn Monroe 88–89
Mistaken for Dead 225
Monkey of Drumlanrig Castle, The 168–171
Monks of St. Bruno, The 43
Mont-Saint-Michel, Normandy, France 120–121
Montgomery Clift 89
Mother Red Cap 191–194
Newgate Prison, London 140, 145
Norfolk Island Ghosts 205
Old Angel Inn, Niagara-on-the-Lake, Ontario, Canada 96
Orient Express 194–195
Orson Welles 92, 125
Paris Catacombs, France 116–117
Peter Rugg 177, 181, 182
Phantom Canoe 216
Phantom City 195
Phantom Fire 238
Piano, The 48
Poltergeists and Puberty 244
Pompeii, Italy 220–221
Port Arthur, Tasmania, Australia 96–100
Prague 108, 110, 113, 116
Premonitions 198–200
Robert E. Lee 62

Rudolph Valentino 77–79
St.Augustine, Florida 127–128
St. Michael's Mount, Cornwall 228–229
Screaming Skull of Bettiscombe Manor, The 234–235
Screaming Tunnel, The, Niagara Falls 96
Shades of Al Capone 238–241
Showers of Stones 245–246
Spectral Hounds 158, 161, 162, 164, 165, 167, 168
Strange Parallels 50
Threave Castle, Dumfriesshire, Scotland 20–21
Tower of London 137, 145, 149, 150, 151, 153, 172
UB65 207, 210, 211
USS *Hornet* 25, 215–216√
Voodoo Queens, The 70–71
Whitby Abbey, Yorkshire, England 106
White Lady of the Hohenzollern 25, 116, 200–201
White Lady of Wolfsegg, The 48–49
White Witch of Jamaica 47–48
Winchester Mansion, San Jose, California 24, 128, 129, 131
Whitby Abbey, North Yorkshire, England 106–107
Windsor Castle, England 56–57
Witch of Endor 74
Castlereagh, Lord 72, 186
Catacombs, Paris 116–117
Chaney, Lon 79–80
Charles Bridge, Prague 108, 110, 113
Chase, Dorcas 230
Cheyne Walk, Chelsea, London 136–138
Chumley's, Bedford Street, Manhattan 125

Church Grim 158
Cleopatra's Needle, London 138–139
Clift, Montgomery 89
Collis, Maurice 244, 245
Cook, Captain James 106
Cook, Florence 69, 70
Cook, Nell 209
Coolidge, Grace 61
Coons, Jonathan 69
Corder, William 225, 226
Crockett, Davy 131
Crookes, Sir William 69, 70
Culloden, Battle of 238

D
Darcy, Thomas 54
Dean, James 86, 88
Deen, Douglas 248, 249
De Feo, Ronald 223, 224, 225
Demarest, D.J. 225
Despard, F.W. 34
Despard, Rosina 35
Doomsday Book 40
Dos Passos, John 125
Douglas, Lady Anne 170
Douglas, William 170
Doyle, Sir Arthur Conan 161
Drayton Church, nr. Uxbridge, London 171
Dudley, John, Duke of Northumberland 150, 151
Duffy, Barney 205
Dundee, Viscount 103
Dunglass, Daniel 72
Durham Castle, England 32–33
Dyer, Amelia 145

E
Edinburgh, Scotland 101, 102, 103, 105, 108
Edinburgh Castle, Scotland 103

Edward III 57
Edward VI 150
Eiffel Tower, Paris, France 30–31
Eliot, George 137
Elizabeth I 150, 153
Empress of Ireland 38
Endor, Witch of 74
Exeter Cathedral, England 22–23
exorcism 249
Exorcist, The 25, 248

F
Faulkner, William 125
Ferreira, Maria José 246
Fitz, John 54
Fitzgerald, Penelope 165
Fitzgerald, Scott 125
Ford, Arthur 75, 76
Fordham University, Manhattan 125
Forest Lawn Memorial Park Cemetery, Glendale, California, 79, 82
Fort Erie, Ontario 96
Fort McNair, Washington, D.C. 46–47
Fox family 43, 45, 46
Foyster, Marianne 43
Frank, Anne 66
Franz Ferdinand, Archduke 201
Frederick II 191
Frederick the Great 201
French and Indian War 96

G
Gable, Clark 80, 81, 82, 83
Gallipoli, Battle of 206
George II 238
Golem of Prague 113, 116
Graceland, Memphis, Tennessee 91
Grey, Lady Jane 149, 150, 151
Guinness, Alec 88
Gunpowder Plot 153
Gwynne, Major John 136

H
Hamilton, Alexander 58, 59
Hamilton, Lady, of Bothwellhaugh 103
Hampton Court, England 139–140
Harlow, Jean 80–82
Harvard University, Cambridge, Massachusetts 52–53
Hatfield House, Hertfordshire, England 12–13
Heartbreak Hotel, Memphis Hotel 89, 91
Henry II 149
Henry VI 149
Henry VIII 57, 134, 139, 149, 150, 153, 156
Herne the Hunter 57
Hilda, St. 106
Hohenzollern 116, 201
    Burg Hohenzollern, Berlin 116
Hollywood Roosevelt Hotel 88, 89
Holyrood House, Palace of 103, 104–105
Houdini, Harry 74–76
Hound of the Baskervilles 158
Howard, Catherine 139, 149
Howard, Lady Mary 54–58
Hudson River Tunnel, 36

J
Jacobite Rising 238
James I 54, 153
James, Frank 63
James, Jesse Woodson 62–64
Jefferson, Thomas 58
Joachim II, Elector 116
Joseph of Arimathea 189
Jumel, Eliza 60

K
Karpis, Alvin 'Creepy' 125
Kelly, George 'Machine-gun' 125

King, John 69
King, Katie 69, 70
Klushi, Franek 29

L
Lake Havasu City, Arizona 122
Lamoureux, Robert 48
Laveau, Marie 70–71
Lee, General Robert E. 62
Liberace 92 93
Lincoln, Abraham 46, 47, 60–61, 62
Lincoln, Mary Todd 60
Loew, Rabbi 113, 116
Loft, Bob 94
Lombard, Carole 82–83
London Underground 36
Lorelei 185
Louis IX 43
Louis XIV 117

M
Manhattan, New York City 123–125
Manson, Charles 81
Marten, Maria 225
Mary Tudor 150
Mary, Queen of Scots 103, 105, 168
mediums 48, 69, 72, 75
Millay, Edna St. Vincent 125
Miller, Arthur 88
Millette, Dorothy 81
Moll Cut-Purse 193
Monckton, Lionel 158, 161
Monroe, Marilyn 88–89
Montague-Douglas-Scott, Lady Alice
  171
Mont-Saint-Michel, Normandy, France
  120
Moon, Sun Myung 50
Mount Carmel Cemetery, Hillside,
  Chicago 85
Mount Olivet Cemetery, Chicago 65, 85

N
Napa County, California 50
Napoleon III 48
National Laboratory of Psychical
  Research, University of London 68
Native Americans 50, 128, 131
Negri, Pola 79
Newby Church, near Ripon, England
  25
Newgate Prison, London 140, 145
Nin, Anaïs 125

O
O'Neill, Eugene 125
Okehampton Castle, Devon, England
  54, 58
Old Bailey, London 140, 145
Olivier, Laurence 88
Order of the Golden Dawn 72
Orlamond, Kunigunde von 116

P
Padfoot 165
Palladino, Eusapia 69
Palmer, Annie 47
Parker, Bonnie 76–77
Peel Castle, Isle of Man, England 164
Penn, Sybil 140
Percy, Thomas 153
Phelps, Reverend E. 244
Pole, Margaret 150
poltergeists 25, 242–249
Port Arthur, Tasmania, Australia
  96–100
Powell, William 81
Powles, Reverend Robert Frazer 156
Prague, Czech Republic 108, 110, 113,
  116
Presley, Elvis 15, 89, 91
Prestbury Church, near Cheltenham,
  England 28

Price, Harry 42, 43, 68
Princes in the Tower, The 149
Pulteney, Sir John de 36

Q
Queen Mary 216, 219, 222
Quantrill's Raiders 63

R
radiant boys 25, 72, 186
Raleigh, Sir Walter 36, 151
Repo, Don 94
Richard II 57
Roosevelt, Theodore 129
Rosma, Charles 45
Royal Circus Hotel, Edinburgh,
  Scotland 103
Royal Society, London 70
Ruffin, Elizabeth 197
Rugg, Peter 177, 181, 182

S
St. Augustine, Florida 127–128
St. Mark's Church, Manhattan 123
St. Mary's Church, Bungay, Suffolk,
  England 161
St. Valentine's Day Massacre 238, 240
St. Vitus's Cathedral, Prague, Czech
  Republic 113
Samuel, Prophet 74
Santa Anna, General 131
Saul, King 74
Seymour, Jane 140
Sheep's Heid, Edinburgh, Scotland 103
Shepherd, Jack 145
Shriker 165
Society for Psychical Research 35, 198
Spinning Jenny 72
Steinbeck, John 125
Stoker, Bram 106
Stuyvesant, Peter 123

Sudbury, Simon 209
Surratt, John Jr. 46, 47
Surratt, Mary 46, 47
Sweet Lady Jane's Restaurant, Los
 Angeles 92
Swifte, Edmund 153
Swinhoe, Henry 34
Swinhoe, Imogen 34, 35

T
Tate, Sharon 81
Terhune, Albert 167
Theatre Royal, Bath, England 171
Thomas, Dylan 85–86
Thorne, John 35
Threave Castle, Dumfriesshire,
 Scotland 20–21
Thurber, James 125
Tintagel Castle 186
Tower of London 137, 145, 149, 150,
 151, 153, 172
Tracy, Spencer 80
Travis, William B. 131, 132
Truman, Harry 61
Twain, Mark 125
Tyler, Wat 209
Tyrone, Lord 25, 200

U
University College, London 64

V
Valentino, Rudolph 77–79
Verasdin, Croatia 238
Versailles 117, 119

W
Walpole, Henry 151
War of 1812 96
Watertown, SS 230
Wawel Castle, Krakow 108

Welles, Orson 92, 125
Wentworth, Thomas 149
Westwood Memorial Cemetery, Los
 Angeles 89
Whitby Abbey, Yorkshire, England 106
White Horse Tavern, Greenwich
 Village, New York 85, 86
White House, Washington, D.C. 60, 61
Whitehead, Sarah 132
Wielopolski, Miss 108
Wight, Isle of 195, 206
Wilhelm II 201
Wilhelmina of the Netherlands 61
Windsor Castle, England 56–57
Wolsey, Cardinal Thomas 139, 149

ACKNOWLEDGEMENTS

Art Directors and TRIP Photo Library/ the following photographers.

© Andrea Alborno: Page 44.
© Martin Barlow: Pages 51, 214.
© Stuart Burgess: Page 142.
© Tibor Bognar: Pages 26, 37, 52, 53, 104, 111, 113, 118, 120.
© David Brooker: Page 12.
© Twink Carter: Page 158.
© Jerry Dennis: Pages 15 left, 90, 91.
© Antonia Deutsch: Page 194 below.
© Judy Drew: Page 190.
© Brian Gibbs: Pages 34. 132, 135, 192.
© Colin Gibson: Pages 109, 160.
© Fiona Good: Page 102.
© Spencer Grant: Pages 6, 79 right, 126, 180, 218, 219, 235.
© Jean Hall: Page 188.
© Richard Hammerton: Page 245.
© David Harding: Pages 103, 194 top.
© Juliet Highlet: Pages 47, 49.
© Douglas Houghton: Pages 18, 191, cover back.
© Ester James: Page 16.
© Mary Jelliffe: Page 70.
© Malcolm Jenkin: Page 217.
© Michael Keep: Page 199.
© Andew Lambert: Page 114.
© Malcolm Lee: Page 84 both.
© Rob Lewis: Page 25 top.
© Barry McGlone: Page 146.
© Ken McLaren: Page 127.
© Paul Petterson: Page 110.
© Clay Perry: Pages 2, 186. cover spine.
© Picturesque Inc.: Page 59.
© John Robertson: Pages 236.
© Helene Rogers: Pages: 24, 32, 55, 66, 100, 101, 116, 117 right, 167, 171 below, 228.
© Brian Seed: Page 88.
© Robin Smith: Pages 26, 97, 98, 99 below, 204, 205.
© Mark Stevenson: Page 10 left, front cover below right.
© Vince Streano & Carol Havens: Page 220.
© Jane Sweeney: Page 246.
© Th-foto Werbung: Page 29 below.
© Constance Toms: Pages 8, 177.
© Flora Torrance: Page 232.

© Adina Tovy: Pages 71, 72, 112, 130, 131, 156, 166, 239.
© Bob Turner: Pages 9, 30, 56, 61 right, 95, 123, 138, 141, 148, 151, 152, 159, 172, 203, 212.
© Geoff Turner: Page 154.
© Brian Vikander: Page 183.
© Joan Wakelin: Pages 99 top, 106.
© Roy Westlake: Page 184.
© Terry Why: Page 234.
© Nick & Janet Wiseman: Page 36.
© Chris Wormald: Pages 22, 178, 181, 187, 195, 196.
© Allan Wright: Pages 20, 168 below, 169.

Diane Canwell & Johathan Sutherland: Pages 64, 161, 162.

© Bettmann/CORBIS: Pages 80, 83, 92, 93, 223, 224, 238, 240.
© CinemaPhoto/CORBIS: Pages 81, 89.
© Hulton-Deutsch Collection/CORBIS: Pages 4, 69, 87, 241.
© Floris Leeuwenberg/The Cover Story/CORBIS: Page 45.
© John Springer Collection/CORBIS: Page 82.
© CORBIS: Page 215.

© Fortean Picture Library: Pages 11, 10 right, 11, 14 left, 19, 25 below, 28 all, 29 top, 40, 42 above, 68 front cover below left.

Library of Congress: Pages 15 right, 46, 58 top left, 60 both, 61 left, 62 all, 63 both, 74, 75 all, 77 right, 79 left, 123 below, 128 both, 129, 149, 198 right, 201 all, 202 both, 210, 222, 231.

© 2004 TopFoto.co.uk: Pages 3, 227, 242, 243, 248, 249.
© 2006 Fortean/TopFoto.co.uk: Page 43, 134, 174, 175, 198 left, 226.
© 2004 TopFoto.co.uk/upp: Page 54.
© 2000 Topham PicturePoint/AP/TopFoto.co.uk: Page 77 left.
© 2004 TopFoto.co.uk/ImageWorks: Page 122.

National Park Service: Pages 94, 171 top, 172 left.

Kevin Oately: Pages 5, 38, 39, 41, 65, 133, 136 both, 137, 144, 163, 164, 165, 168 top, 193.

©Nick Rains-PPL

Regency House Publishing Ltd: Pages 58 top right and below, 78, 85, 86, 123 above, 124, 125, 139, 170, front cover top.

ACKNOWLEDGEMENTS

Art Directors and TRIP Photo Library/ the following photographers.

© Andrea Alborno: Page 44.
© Martin Barlow: Pages 51, 214.
© Stuart Burgess: Page 142.
© Tibor Bognar: Pages 26, 37, 52, 53, 104, 111, 113, 118, 120.
© David Brooker: Page 12.
© Twink Carter: Page 158.
© Jerry Dennis: Pages 15 left, 90, 91.
© Antonia Deutsch: Page 194 below.
© Judy Drew: Page 190.
© Brian Gibbs: Pages 34. 132, 135, 192.
© Colin Gibson: Pages 109, 160.
© Fiona Good: Page 102.
© Spencer Grant: Pages 6, 79 right, 126, 180, 218, 219, 235.
© Jean Hall: Page 188.
© Richard Hammerton: Page 245.
© David Harding: Pages 103, 194 top.
© Juliet Highlet: Pages 47, 49.
© Douglas Houghton: Pages 18, 191, cover back.
© Ester James: Page 16.
© Mary Jelliffe: Page 70.
© Malcolm Jenkin: Page 217.
© Michael Keep: Page 199.
© Andew Lambert: Page 114.
© Malcolm Lee: Page 84 both.
© Rob Lewis: Page 25 top.
© Barry McGlone: Page 146.
© Ken McLaren: Page 127.
© Paul Petterson: Page 110.
© Clay Perry: Pages 2, 186. cover spine.
© Picturesque Inc.: Page 59.
© John Robertson: Pages 236.
© Helene Rogers: Pages: 24, 32, 55, 66, 100, 101, 116, 117 right, 167, 171 below, 228.
© Brian Seed: Page 88.
© Robin Smith: Pages 26, 97, 98, 99 below, 204, 205.
© Mark Stevenson: Page 10 left, front cover below right.
© Vince Streano & Carol Havens: Page 220.
© Jane Sweeney: Page 246.
© Th-foto Werbung: Page 29 below.
© Constance Toms: Pages 8, 177.
© Flora Torrance: Page 232.

© Adina Tovy: Pages 71, 72, 112, 130, 131, 156, 166, 239.
© Bob Turner: Pages 9, 30, 56, 61 right, 95, 123, 138, 141, 148, 151, 152, 159, 172, 203, 212.
© Geoff Turner: Page 154.
© Brian Vikander: Page 183.
© Joan Wakelin: Pages 99 top, 106.
© Roy Westlake: Page 184.
© Terry Why: Page 234.
© Nick & Janet Wiseman: Page 36.
© Chris Wormald: Pages 22, 178, 181, 187, 195, 196.
© Allan Wright: Pages 20, 168 below, 169.

Diane Canwell & Johnathan Sutherland: Pages 64, 161, 162.

© Bettmann/CORBIS: Pages 80, 83, 92, 93, 223, 224, 238, 240.
© CinemaPhoto/CORBIS: Pages 81, 89.
© Hulton-Deutsch Collection/CORBIS: Pages 4, 69, 87, 241.
© Floris Leeuwenberg/The Cover Story/CORBIS: Page 45.
© John Springer Collection/CORBIS: Page 82.
© CORBIS: Page 215.

© Fortean Picture Library: Pages 11, 10 right, 11, 14 left, 19, 25 below, 28 all, 29 top, 40, 42 above, 68 front cover below left.

Library of Congress: Pages 15 right, 46, 58 top left, 60 both, 61 left, 62 all, 63 both, 74, 75 all, 77 right, 79 left, 123 below, 128 both, 129, 149, 198 right, 201 all, 202 both, 210, 222, 231.

© 2004 TopFoto.co.uk: Pages 3, 227, 242, 243, 248, 249.
© 2006 Fortean/TopFoto.co.uk: Page 43, 134, 174, 175, 198 left, 226.
© 2004 TopFoto.co.uk/upp: Page 54.
© 2000 Topham PicturePoint/AP/TopFoto.co.uk: Page 77 left.
© 2004 TopFoto.co.uk/ImageWorks: Page 122.

National Park Service: Pages 94, 171 top, 172 left.

Kevin Oately: Pages 5, 38, 39, 41, 65, 133, 136 both, 137, 144, 163, 164, 165, 168 top, 193.

©Nick Rains-PPL

Regency House Publishing Ltd: Pages 58 top right and below, 78, 85, 86, 123 above, 124, 125, 139, 170, front cover top.